ADDICTIONS:
GAMBLING, SMOKING,
COCAINE USE, AND OTHERS

ADDICTIONS:
GAMBLING, SMOKING,
COCAINE USE, AND OTHERS

MARGARET O. HYDE

McGRAW-HILL BOOK COMPANY

NEW YORK   ST. LOUIS   SAN FRANCISCO

AUCKLAND   BOGOTÁ   DÜSSELDORF   JOHANNESBURG

LONDON   MADRID   MEXICO   MONTREAL

NEW DELHI   PANAMA   PARIS   SÃO PAULO   SINGAPORE

SYDNEY   TOKYO   TORONTO

Library of Congress Cataloging in Publication Data

Hyde, Margaret Oldroyd, date.
  Gambling, smoking, cocaine use, and other addictions.

    Bibliography: p.
    Includes index.
    1. Gambling.   2.   Smoking.   3.   Drug abuse.
I.   Title.
HV6710.H9   362.2'9   77-17024
ISBN 0-07-031645-7

  3456789 MUBP 7832109

TO CHRISTINE B. REICHARD
AND WINFIELD P. REICHARD

CONTENTS

.

ACKNOWLEDGMENTS

The author wishes to thank the many people who contributed information and suggestions for this book. The following people were especially helpful:

—Peter G. Bourne, M.D., Special Assistant to the President for health issues
—Sydney Cohen, M.D., Vista Hill Foundation, San Diego, California
—Ron Dubren, Ph.D., American Health Foundation, New York City
—Arlene Fonaroff, M.P.H, Ph.D., Committee on Substance Abuse and Habitual Behavior, National Research Council, Washington, D.C.
—Elizabeth Forsyth, M.D., psychiatrist, Burlington, Vermont
—William Glasser, Institute for Reality Therapy, Los Angeles, California
—Alida Glen, Ph.D., Veterans Administration Hospital, Cleveland, Ohio

—Abe S. Kramer, M.D., Veterans Administration Hospital, Fort Hamilton, Brooklyn, New York

—Tomas Martinez, Ph.D., University of Colorado, Boulder, Colorado

—Marie Nyswander, M.D., Rockefeller University, New York City

—Vic Pawlak, Do It Now Foundation, Phoenix, Arizona

—Stanley Schachter, Ph.D., Columbia University, New York City

—Lester Soyka, M.D., University of Vermont Medical College, Burlington, Vermont

—Kenneth Stroup, National Organization for the Reform of Marijuana Laws, Washington, D.C.

—Alfred J. Vent, M.S.W, C.S.W., Psychiatric Services Center, White Plains, New York

If you were asked to describe an addict, your description could vary a great deal and still fit one of the many definitions that are currently being used. Today, one talks about food addicts, coffee addicts, and people who are addicted to gambling. The heavy smoker who tries to break the habit often refers to his or her "addiction" to cigarettes. Only a small percentage of the people who drink alcohol are addicted to it, but alcoholism is a well-recognized addiction. Is the workaholic an addict? Actually, addiction may not involve drugs. It is not a mysterious chemical process, but a characteristic of a person's way of dealing with life. Jogging, cycling, and meditation are considered addicting, by broad definitions. One might include a long list of substances and activities that qualify as addictions, since people's behavior toward them is a major part of the concept.

Using broad definitions for addictions is not new. For many years, *addiction* was the term used in connection with habits, both good and bad. Nonsubstance-related behaviors that have been viewed traditionally as addictive are work, sports, and child rearing. The *Oxford English Dictionary* defines addiction as "a state of being (self-) addicted or given to a habit or pursuit; devotion." Another definition in the same dictionary is "the way in which one is addicted; inclination; bent; leaning; penchant." In this dictionary, drugs are not mentioned in the definitions for addiction.

The diagnosis for drug addiction was not officially recognized in the United States until 1934, when it was included for the first time in the American Psychiatric Association's publication, *Standard Classified Nomenclature of Diseases*. Here it was placed among kinds of mental illnesses and considered as one kind. For the next few decades, especially when there was much talk about drug abuse, *addiction* generally referred to narcotic addiction and an *addict* was considered a heroin addict. But even the "addict in the street" no longer can be described as the typical addict, for investigation shows that there is no typical addict, even when one confines the definition to the use of heroin.

One popular contemporary definition of drug addiction describes it as follows: "a state of periodic or chronic intoxication, detrimental to the individual and to society, produced by repeated consumption of a drug . . ." This definition was created by the World Health Organization in 1965, but even then authorities questioned the use of the word *intoxication* in refer-ence to heroin. They also questioned whether or not the controlled use of an opiate would qualify as addiction under this definition, since a person using morphine to relieve pain could hardly be called det-rimental to society. But a patient on regular doses of morphine would qualify as an addict by other defini-tions.

The term *tolerance* is commonly used in defini-tions of addiction. Tolerance is the need for increasing amounts of a substance to produce the same effect on the body with regular use. For example, several cups of coffee may be needed to produce the same effect as one cup after the body becomes more tolerant to the caffeine in the coffee. Tolerance differs both with drugs and with the individuals who take them. Com-pare tolerance for narcotics such as morphine, heroin, opium, and codeine with alcohol tolerance. Only a small proportion of people who drink alcohol become dependent on it to the extent that they are considered addicted. A very high percentage of heroin users be-come addicted, and about 70 percent of morphine users become addicted. Those people who continue both of these drugs to the point of addiction show increased tolerance, but the degree of increase varies greatly. In the case of alcohol, tolerance increases amounts to only three to four times the original inher-ent tolerance, but in the case of opiates there is a twenty-five- to one-hundred-fold rise. Tolerance may be a condition in which body cells protect themselves against toxic substances by developing resistance to them.

In addition to a tendency to increase the dose because of tolerance, another hallmark of addiction is a compulsive need to continue to take the drug or indulge in the habit. When the word *compulsive* is applied to negative behavioral patterns, it means that they are characterized by the continual commitment of an act that violates a person's standards. The compulsion is a craving, or a command from within. A repetitive thought enters the mind of an addicted person, and there is a feeling that the thought must be acted out. In both positive and negative addictions, frustration and irritability are characteristic of not acting upon these inner commands. A runner who is addicted to spending an hour in his favorite exercise every day feels frustrated and irritable when he or she cannot run as usual. A compulsive gambler will continue no matter what the risk. For this person gambling has become so irresistible that it asserts itself before family needs and personal safety. But with gambling there is no physiological factor. An alcoholic who cannot stop drinking is influenced by psychological and social factors much as a gambler is, but here a physiological or biochemical factor is involved too. So it is with many other kinds of addiction. Craving may go hand in hand with the physiological dependence, but it may be far more than physiological.

Craving is often considered the central and defining characteristic of addiction, with the instinct to relapse existing in a latent or unconscious form. If a person who has broken an addictive habit is suddenly exposed to appropriate temptations or circumstances, there is a high risk that s/he will return to the old habit. The theory that locking an addict away from the source of supply or from an environment such as a gambling casino does not work. People who have been in jail for years have been known to return to their addictions as soon as they are released.

When the craving involves physical dependence, the idea of separating an addict from a drug is especially popular among those who do not look deeply at the problem of addiction. Some people believe that if an addict suffers withdrawal, or unpleasant physical symptoms, the addiction will end. A promise to stay away from the cause of the withdrawal symptoms is often extracted from an addict. The end of the addiction cycle might be expected to come when the body is forced to function without the presence of the drug to which it has become adjusted. While this may be the case in a relatively small percentage of cases, craving and psychological factors play a part in most addictions.

Although physical withdrawal is an important characteristic in many definitions of addiction, it is but one factor. Withdrawal differs in symptoms and severity, depending on a number of things such as kind of drug, kind of habit, amount of tolerance, and the medical care that is available. Some addicts never suffer from withdrawal because they live in a controlled situation.

By now, it is evident that defining addiction is difficult since addiction means so many things to different people. One definition does not satisfy all cases. In addition to this, ideas are constantly changing. Consider the case of Dr. Maurice Partridge, a consultant psychiatrist to St. George's Hospital and the Royal Marsden Hospital in London. About ten years ago, Dr. Partridge was asked to speak at the New York Medical College on the subject of addiction. This English doctor opened his speech by explaining that he was somewhat disconcerted at being asked to talk about addiction since drug addiction in Great Britain had hardly existed until recently. He reported that there was an average of 336 narcotic addicts annually between the years 1936 and 1960. About 75 percent of these were believed to be "respectable" middle-aged or elderly people who started taking opiates such as morphine in the course of medical treatment. The other 25 percent were thought to be mostly doctors, nurses, pharmacists, dentists, and other health workers who had easy access to drugs.

Was Dr. Partridge naive? No, he explained that careful records were kept. He himself had reason to observe this in the following situation: A patient, an elderly male traveler, approached Dr. Partridge for a prescription for ten grains of morphine. This man was accustomed to taking small amounts daily and had done so for a period of fifteen years. He wanted just enough to tide him over his brief stay in London and his journey home. Far away, in his home town, he was an executive in a vast commercial undertaking that had its own medical and hospital services, and he could obtain his supply with ease. Since it was obvious to Dr. Partridge that refusing the man would play no part in rehabilitating him, he wrote the prescription, but the doctor later was severely chastised for not going through regular channels, when his unusual behavior came to the attention of the record keepers.

Few people today believe that one can keep an accurate account of narcotic addicts in Great Britain or in the United States. A 1977 report estimates there are 800,000 heroin addicts in the United States. Since this represents just one kind of addiction in one type of geographical location, it is obvious that addiction is widespread.

There has been much confusion about the definition of drug addiction. The World Health Organization's Expert Committee on Addiction Producing Drugs defined drug addiction as: a state of periodic or chronic intoxication produced by the repeated consumption of a drug; and involving tolerance, psychological dependence, usually physical dependence, an overwhelming compulsion to continue using the drug, and detrimental effects on both the individual and society when it is used in spite of its limitations.*

*"Drug Dependence: Its Significance and Characteristics", *World Health Organization Bulletin*, 32: 721–723, 1965.

At one time, the World Health Organization Committee suggested the use of the term *drug dependence* to replace the term *addiction*. *Drug dependence* can be defined as a state sometimes psychic and sometimes physical, arising from repeated administration of a drug on a periodic and continued basis. This definition serves for certain drugs, but the concept of addiction is far more inclusive than dependence, so the term *addiction* remains popular.

While narcotics of the opiate variety, along with certain other drugs, may fit the definition *dependence*, what about the types of addiction that do not involve drugs? And even in the case of those which do, there is some confusion. Not all types of alcoholism are addictive. In the condition known as *alpha alcoholism*, there is a purely psychological dependence on the effect of alcohol. But according to the views of some authorities, the addictive types of alcoholism involve loss of control and inability to abstain.

Much controversy exists about whether certain addictions should be considered diseases or characteristic behaviors that a person uses to deal with the problems in his or her life. How important are childhood experiences? What part does personality play? Does present environment help to determine whether or not a person will become an addict?

Some authorities argue strongly that addiction is not a disease based on biochemical phenomena but is a behavioral problem. Others claim changes or differences in physical makeup prove it is a disease.

Theories of addiction are almost as plentiful as definitions. Even though the word may be hard to define, the condition not only exists, but it is widespread. Exploring the meanings and the causes of addiction is an important way of preventing undesirable addictions and of developing positive addictions such as running and meditation.

Do you know anyone who has tried to stop smoking? While many people have success, at least for a short period of time, there are others who cannot control the urge to smoke no matter how serious the consequences. One man at a New York State hospital who had lung cancer continued to smoke for ten years. Then he developed cancer in the other lung and died. Another patient is reported to have made a device so that he could smoke through the hole in his neck after his cancerous larynx had been removed.

People who want to stop smoking spend millions of dollars on workshops, new products, books, and therapy in an effort to cure their habit. Education has done much to make smokers realize the health hazards to which they are exposing themselves. Many people know that lung cancer is the leading cancer killer among American men. The rate of lung cancer for women is increasing with the rising rate of smoking among women; so that the ratio of male to female deaths from lung cancer has changed from nearly

7-to-1 to 4-to-1. This is not because male deaths have declined but because women are smoking more.

Dr. R. Lee Clark, president of the American Cancer Society, believes that lung cancer is largely preventable. While environmental pollution contributes to the cause of lung cancer, smoking cigarettes is considered the greatest factor. For example, of the 85,000 Americans expected to die this year as the result of lung cancer, it is estimated that 80 percent of these deaths will be due to smoking. In all kinds of cancer deaths, about one in every five is blamed on smoking.

Smoking is also considered an agent in diseases of the circulatory system, including heart disease and high blood pressure. Cigarette smoking sets in motion physiological changes that cause the walls of the heart to contract more strongly and more frequently. This increases the heart's need for oxygen and other nutrients, but smoking, which caused this change, also decreases the oxygen supply by about 10 percent. Thus a smoker's heart needs more oxygen and gets less. Carbon monoxide in cigarette smoke is responsible for some of this problem. While nicotine has been shown to be the habit-former, carbon monoxide, which comprises as much as 5 percent of tobacco smoke, is one of the many toxic substances that are inhaled. There is much concern about unventilated filter tips with nonporous paper around the filter, preventing the dilution of inhaled smoke by air through the cigarette wall. Chronic heavy exposure to carbon monoxide appears to promote the initial development of atherosclerosis (hardening of the arteries) and cause other circulatory problems. Lung impairment, often caused by heavy smoking, also decreases the supply of oxygen to the heart.

"Tar" is the common name for the particulate matter found in cigarette smoke. Laboratory studies have isolated a number of chemical compounds that cause cancer from tobacco smoke. In addition to this, there are elements in the smoke which interact with other compounds to promote cancer production.

A chest specialist at an American Medical Association convention remarked that people who get lung cancer from smoking are lucky in comparison with those who get emphysema. Many tiny air sacs in the lungs of emphysema sufferers have been destroyed. Since this is where oxygen goes into the body, a person with emphysema has difficulty breathing; and the disease grows progressively worse. A normal adult when resting uses about 5 percent of total energy in breathing; a person with emphysema uses as much as 80 percent. It is very exhausting. This kind of breathing has been compared to the gasping of a fish out of water.

In spite of the knowledge that smoking is a major factor in lung cancer, other cancers, circulatory diseases, emphysema, and other lung disorders, a great many people continue to smoke. And although 30 million Americans have stopped smoking since the antismoking campaigns began in 1964, 55 to 60 million Americans are still smoking. Nineteen sixty-four was the year of the Surgeon General's Report. Its most significant conclusions follow:

"Cigarette smoking is a health hazard of sufficient importance to warrant remedial action."

"Cigarette smoking is causally related to lung cancer in men; the magnitude of the effect of cigarette smoking far outweighs other factors. The data for women, although less extensive, points in the same direction."

After this there was a drop in cigarette sales, but even though further scientific evidence was amassed, the drop was short-lived. Congress enacted the first national law regulating the labeling of cigarettes; nevertheless, today few smokers pay much attention to the label on each pack that states: "WARNING: THE SURGEON GENERAL HAS DETERMINED THAT CIGARETTE SMOKING IS DANGEROUS TO YOUR HEALTH."

What produces the craving for cigarettes that causes so many people to smoke in spite of their awareness of the risks? There are many toxic substances in cigarette smoke, but nicotine appears to be the one that causes the habit. Confirmed smokers act with a compulsion that has been compared to that of the heroin addict. While the role of nicotine in smoking is not completely clear, it is an addicting drug that produces a strange combination of effects. When smokers need stimulation, they perceive the smoke as stimulating. When they are tense, smoking appears to have a relaxing effect. This is not just imagined. Experiments with nicotine show its effect on the body.

Many interesting experiments have been carried out to study nicotine. In large amounts, nicotine is known to be fatal. At least one case of murder by nicotine has been reported, in which a man killed his brother by dropping pure nicotine on his tongue. The lethal dose is about 30 milligrams. Only about 1 milligram reaches the bloodstream when smoking one cigarette, but it does so rapidly. Actually, absorption, metabolism, and elimination of nicotine take place so fast that a person's blood level of nicotine is usually reduced by half in about 20 minutes; elimination of most other drugs proceeds much more slowly. The pattern of many dependent smokers is a cigarette about every 30 minutes. It is not surprising that this coincides with the time interval needed to keep a high level of nicotine in the brain, and may explain the frequency of smoking of those who are dependent on it.

Not all experts agree that nicotine is an addictive drug, however. For some people, due to individual reactions, it may not be. Still, according to *Licit and Illicit Drugs: The Consumers Union Report on Narcotics, Stimulants, Depressants, Inhalants, Hallucinogens and Marijuana—including Caffeine, Nicotine, and Alcohol*, nicotine is one of the most perniciously addicting drugs in common use. Edward M. Brecher and the editors of Consumer Reports, who authored the book, believe that most tobacco users are "hooked."

Becoming addicted to nicotine through cigarette smoking is easier than becoming dependent on alcohol or barbiturates, according to some experts. While intermittent or occasional use is common with many drugs, occasional cigarette smoking is typical for only a small percentage of smokers.

In the arguments about whether or not nicotine is addicting, the subject of tolerance points toward a positive answer. Few, if any, people enjoy the taste of their first cigarette. Many adolescents try one cigarette, decide they do not like smoking, and never try again. But others, for a variety of psychological and social reasons, smoke more cigarettes. It is believed that few stop smoking after the third or fourth cigarette. The first cigarette is not well tolerated, but as tolerance rises, a person may smoke several cigarettes in one day without the toxic effects of pallor, nausea, sweating, etc. As tolerance increases, the body can cope with as much as two packs a day, but even ten cigarettes would produce illness in a beginner. Dr. Hamilton Russell of the Addiction Research Unit of the Institute of Psychiatry in London has studied the addicting effects of nicotine quite extensively and has shown physiological changes that take place as tolerance to nicotine develops. But other factors than nicotine are involved in the cigarette habit. This is evident since nicotine in tablet form is rarely, if ever, abused.

Withdrawal is another characteristic of true addiction that appears to be present in the case of nicotine. Drowsiness, headaches, digestive upsets, nervousness, insomnia, tremors, and fatigue are among the symptoms reported in studies of smokers who were deprived of the drug nicotine.

Dr. Stanley Schachter, a Columbia University psychologist, reports that almost any smoker can give a believable reason for smoking. Many people say that they smoke for pleasure, relaxation, or something to do with their hands. Others believe they smoke because they have oral problems that are left over from childhood. Dr. Schachter believes that heavy smokers have only *one* real reason for their cigarette habits and that reason is nicotine addiction. He and his colleagues have conducted a number of experiments with smokers over a period of four years. In one experiment, they found that heavy smokers who were given low-tar, low-nicotine cigarettes tried to compensate for the reduced amount of nicotine by puffing more frequently and by smoking a greater number of cigarettes. This appeared to be an effort to obtain their normal amount of nicotine. The smokers who were not able to do so with the new brand showed withdrawal symptoms such as irritability and poor concentration.

Dr. Schachter and his team carried out experiments with smokers who were experiencing withdrawal to discover how they acted under stress. Conclusions indicated that *not* smoking increases anxiety because of withdrawal. Smokers claim that cigarettes reduce tension, but they may actually feel this way because smoking prevents the tension that builds with withdrawal. Dr. Schachter is not prejudiced by being a nonsmoker. He claims that it is possible for him to stop smoking only if he is willing to put up with the withdrawal.

While most smokers wish they had not started and report that they want to stop, many do not because they find it quite difficult to give up their habit. People who say they do not have "addictive personalities" and will not "get hooked" on nicotine may be surprised to find that the most stable, well-adjusted people can become addicted if they smoke for even a short period of time.

While a dramatic decline in percentages of smokers in the general population has been noted for the years 1970 to 1975, there has been an increase among teenage girls (ages 13 to 17) and young women (ages 18 to 35 years). Half a million more teenage girls are smoking now than a few years ago. An American Cancer Society study showed that 22 percent of all teenage girls smoked in 1969 and 27 percent smoked in the findings reported in 1976. There was also an increase in the number of cigarettes smoked by this age group, with four out of ten girls smoking as much as one pack a day in the most recent study. While the incidence of smoking among young women has increased only slightly, those who smoke do so more often.

Why is there such an increase when this group of girls and young women are aware of the hazards? There is little question as to whether or not the health message has been heard, since most of this group agrees that smoking is harmful. More than half of the young smokers questioned believe wholly, or in part, that smoking is as addictive as some illegal drugs. A study about cigarette smoking among teenage girls and young women conducted for the American Cancer Society reported in 1976 that peer relationships continue to operate as a dominant influence. Among smokers, it was found that 82 percent of all teenage girls think of teenagers as smokers rather than nonsmokers and 66 percent say that at least half of their friends smoke. Of this group, 84 percent of the fathers smoke or did smoke at one time. Sixty-four percent of the mothers were either smokers or had smoked in the past. This was indication that a smoking environment appears to encourage young people to begin smoking.

In addition to the part played by a smoking environment, other factors seem to be involved in whether or not a young person begins to smoke. About half the nonsmokers abstain because they are strongly religious and/or respectful of authority. This half shies away from those who smoke and those who are influenced by new values. The remainder of the nonsmokers are quite different. They are exposed to a smoking environment and accept many of the new values, but they have strong feelings against smoking. This group emphasizes physical fitness and is concerned about the addictive nature of cigarettes. They find new peer identification by backing the cause of antismoking. They are militant nonsmokers who try to increase regulations for nonsmoking areas.

Smoking among teenage boys remains at about the same level that it has been for a number of years. About 30 percent of the boys smoke. Their reasons for beginning to smoke are much the same as the girls' except that for them, smoking plays more of a part in the need to be popular and in their feelings about themselves than it does with girls. For a small percentage of both boys and girls, rebelling against authority plays a part.

More girls than boys have tried to quit smoking. One reason for this appears to be that the boy smokers are more apt to think of smoking as a social asset. The girls may be more eager to stop because they are more apprehensive about the health hazards, cigarette odor, and possible harm to future children. The dangers of smoking to unborn children is clear. Carbon monoxide reduces the capacity of the blood to carry oxygen to the body and in turn reduces the supply of oxygen to an unborn baby. Pregnant women who smoke are more likely to have babies that are underweight. Heavy smoking in combination with other factors such as poor maternal nutrition is believed to double an infant's odds of dying within a month after birth. Even without other negative factors, babies of smoking mothers suffer more chest infections than other infants. Girls who smoke often think about the problems of stopping long before they become pregnant and try to quit so they will not have to deal with giving up cigarettes later.

Even though it is fairly well known that those who start smoking earliest have the greatest chance of relapse when they try to break the habit, six out of ten smokers begin before their thirteenth birthday. Health hazards that do not appear until years later have little meaning to most preteen boys and girls, and anti-smoking programs do not reach them until they are in sixth, seventh, and eighth grades; too late to influence any decision about whether or not to start.

What is the best way to stop smoking? This is a question many people ask and one to which there are many answers. The Smoker's Self-Testing Kit developed by Dr. Daniel Horn, director of the National Clearinghouse for Smoking and Health of the Public Health Service, and members of his staff helps people who want to stop smoking. The kit is designed to help one decide whether or not one wants to give up smoking, to give one some understanding of the problems involved, and to provide some guidelines on how to meet these problems. There are tests that help smokers analyze their real feelings about smoking, and tests that give some insight into the kind of smokers they are and suggestions for quitting based on this identification. The Smoker's Self-Testing Kit is available from the Superintendent of Documents, U.S. Government Printing Office, Washington D.C. 20402, at a cost of $.25. Ask for DHEW publication number (CDC) 74-8716. [Minimum orders from this office are $1.00.]

Some of the reasons both sexes give for wanting to change their smoking habits include: the desire for a better feeling of well-being, to get rid of cigarette breath and odor, and to save money. Although aware of health hazards, many tend to believe this cannot happen to them or to think that air pollution is more likely to give them cancer than cigarettes. Of course, both of these ideas are incorrect.

The type of smoker a person is plays a part in how easy it will be to stop. For some people, handling a cigarette plays an important part in their enjoyment of smoking. For them, substituting toying with a pen or pencil, a piece of jewelry, a coin, or other object helps break the habit. For those who experience a sense of increased energy from smoking, a brisk walk or other moderate exercise is suggested as a replacement. Many smokers who use cigarettes to enhance pleasurable feelings can find substitutes in physical activities, or other social activities such as eating or drinking, as long as these are kept within reasonable bounds. For those who use cigarettes as a tranquilizer in times of stress, similar substitutes may help. The person who smokes heavily in an effort to help deal with problems effectively may discover, on examination, that the smoking does not really help and that smoking or quitting is not an important factor in problem solving.

Some smokers light cigarettes frequently without realizing that they do so. The person who lights a cigarette, puts it in an ashtray, then lights another without realizing there is one in the ashtray is a typical habitual smoker. For this kind of smoker, changing brands and cutting down gradually appear to be effective if they are done with an awareness of the habit element. Rules for breaking habits of any variety help, such as changing the way the cigarettes are smoked and the conditions under which they are smoked. The behavior of habit smoking must be unlearned or a new habit must replace it. Asking "Do I really want this cigarette?" helps. Wrapping the pack so that one must go to the trouble of unwrapping it, or not carrying cigarettes and matches, may help this type of smoker.

For a person whose craving begins the moment a cigarette is put out, stopping "cold turkey" rather than slowing down is advised. In contrast to the smoker described earlier, this smoker is almost always aware of *not* smoking. Since nicotine withdrawal symptoms are unpleasant, quitting may be very difficult. Some addicted smokers find it helpful to smoke more than the usual number of cigarettes for a few days before quitting day so that they no longer enjoy the taste of cigarettes. Then, when the last cigarette has been extinguished, this person must suffer the discomfort of going without nicotine until the body adjusts itself.

The American Health Foundation, a nonprofit organization, has explored a wide range of smoking-cessation activities in its program of disease prevention. Dr. Ron Dubren, head of the Smoking Cessation Division, suggests that those who are going to join a program change brands before they join and set a quitting day as soon as possible after the program starts. The following techniques are used in various combinations in their many programs:

Substitute Activity: Sucking on candy, chewing gum, fondling buttons or matchsticks, etc., are activities that provide substitutes for the missed activity of smoking. This technique is used in all varieties of programs.

Gradual Dosage Reduction: A number of modifications of this technique help individuals lower their smoking dosage; many would-be failures are able to quit this way.

One technique that has made it easier for some smokers to stop is called *stepping down*. By switching brands and reducing nicotine intake in stages, one can *gradually* reduce the body's dependence on nicotine. Some people try this in such rapid stages that they find themselves smoking more cigarettes. For them, the total intake of nicotine is not really reduced. If this has happened to you, try a more gradual drop in nicotine.

Jim was smoking thirty high-nicotine content cigarettes per day. By obtaining a list of brands published by the Federal Trade Commission, "Survey of Tar and Nicotine Content," he moved from the high-nicotine category to the medium-high category, and smoked that brand for three days before stepping down to another category. After a week, he had reached the low-nicotine category, and four days later went to very low-nicotine cigarettes. Although he found these cigarettes less satisfying and he smoked a few extra cigarettes each day, Jim knew that they had about ten times less nicotine than his original brand. He knew that these few extra cigarettes would not offset the advantage he had gained.

Through brand switching, Jim could feel himself becoming less dependent on nicotine. The craving he experienced the first thing every morning was not as great. Now Jim could see the benefits of stepping down and was ready to tackle a day without cigarettes. Even if he never got beyond the first day, he was still ahead. He would never go back to the fist brand with their high-nicotine content.

The American Health Foundation, 1370 Avenue of the Americas, New York, New York 10019, publishes a pamphlet, "Stepping Down from the Habit," which includes a list of brand names with categories of nicotine per cigarette similar to the one mentioned above. Lists are also available from other organizations concerned with smoking.

Situational, Associational, and Event Control: These are techniques that help smokers to think about each cigarette before lighting it. Many people reach for a cigarette from a pack while already smoking another one. Breaking this sort of reflex action may be accomplished by wrapping the pack or placing cigarettes so that they are less available than usual. Breaking the association of environmental stimuli such as coffee, dessert, and television may be accomplished by having the person limit smoking to a specific room where none of these are present. The purpose of this technique is to help the person cut down the frequency of smoking by breaking the typical reinforcement pattern to which the smoker is habituated.

Relaxation—Deep Breathing: Substituting a method of dealing with tension for the practice of smoking has helped many individuals who are giving up their cigarette habits. One technique that is easily practiced is relaxation through deep breathing. The procedure typically suggested in smoking-cessation programs of the American Health Foundation is deep breathing for twenty minutes a day during a period of one or two weeks. After this period, participants practice relaxing their muscles at will. Once mastered, the technique can be used to reduce tension where once the cigarette was used.

As mentioned earlier, the withdrawal process itself may be the cause of tension. This technique is a possible approach whether the tension is from withdrawal or from other causes.

Behavioral Contracting: One of the reasons some smokers give for wanting to stop smoking is the desire to be in control of their own lives. Some people resent the power that "some tobacco wrapped in paper" has over them. The use of behavioral contracts, written plans to abide by certain behavior patterns, appears to be especially helpful for them. It also is especially helpful for people who find it difficult to give up smoking in social situations such as parties. A typical behavioral contract might be one that limits the party smoker to smoking only in the lavatory. If the contract is broken, the person might penalize himself or herself by staying away from the next party. These contracts must be worked out between the smoker and the person who is helping the smoker to stop.

Ex-Smoker Witness: This technique is popular with a variety of programs for those who want to give up their addictions. In the case of smoking, an ex-smoker can help to make the goal more obtainable by example and by providing information about problems s/he had after the cessation program was over. For example, ex-smokers can help by telling how they deal with "needling" by friends who continue to smoke.

Buddy System: This familiar technique helps in smoking cessation. Two people who want to stop take some responsibility for each other, providing mutual support and encouragement. This usually helps to increase motivation and maintain progress.

Systematic Desensitization: Many smokers and ex-smokers have especially strong cravings at certain times. A list of situations is made by the person who is giving up smoking according to the degree of discomfort caused by not smoking. For example, an individual might find not smoking after meals the most difficult time; the craving might be next greatest at a coffee break, slightly less at bedtime, and so on. Beginning with the bottom of the list, the individual is asked to imagine not smoking in the least difficult situation. One by one, the situations are imagined as the imaginary ladder is climbed. When discomfort is experienced, or there is a desire to smoke, the person is instructed to breathe deeply for relaxation or use whatever other technique has been developed. When this technique, known as systematic desensitization, is used with a group, everyone participates in the relaxation procedure each time anyone signals the desire to smoke.

Group Therapy: In the American Health Foundation programs that combine group therapy with other techniques that are mentioned earlier, one leader meets with ten to fifteen people for five weekly meetings. Each meeting lasts ninety minutes, during which time there is no smoking. Coffee is served during the meetings, giving members the experience of enjoying coffee without the cigarettes that they usually smoke at coffee time. Meetings provide structure for behavior change, and the fact that quitting techniques are individual matters is emphasized. While each person examines why, when, and how he or she smokes, group interaction is encouraged so that members can help each other stop. Throughout the five sessions, new directions for a life-style without smoking are put into action. Continued support is supplied by an outline for the year after the therapy program, and some members make use of the buddy system by making arrangements with another member of their group.

Individual Counseling: This technique deals with the same issues as group therapy, with programs lasting from three to five weeks. A support system is set up for the person to follow after the program is completed.

The American Health Foundation is exploring a wide range of programs that includes the above techniques, as well as others, in an effort to identify the amount and type of help needed by individual smokers and to provide a range of programs that will help as many groups of smokers as possible. In addition to matching programs to individuals, new programs are being explored. The separate problem of helping those who have stopped smoking is recognized.

Many people who complete treatment courses in various smoking clinics resume cigarette smoking within six months. Experts do not consider a smoker cured of the cigarette habit until there has been abstinence for at least two years.

While no form or amount of smoking is as safe as not smoking at all, recent studies have indicated that consistent use of low tar/low nicotine in place of higher-rated brands can benefit smokers in three ways: (1) They can reduce the amount of cigarette tar, which is considered the primary cause of smoking-related cancer. (2) They can reduce the exposure to carbon monoxide, one toxic by-product of tobacco that is linked with cardiovascular disorders such as hardening of the arteries (atherosclerosis) and emphysema. Tests indicate that *very* low tar/low nicotine brands yield substantially lower carbon monoxide levels. (3) The degree of addiction is lowered because the amount of nicotine is lowered.

Joe Cattano, smoking specialist of the Multiple Risk Intervention Trial Program of the American Health Foundation, notes that as helpful and promising as low tar/low nicotine brands may appear to the smoker, there is a critical issue that must be understood, and that issue is smoking behavior. The advantage of those brands is negated if: (1) there is an increase in the number of cigarettes smoked; (2) there is an increase in the number of puffs per cigarette; (3) the cigarette is smoked to a shorter butt; and/or (4) there is an increase in the size of each puff. In order to gain the advantage of low tar/low nicotine cigarettes, the smoker must retain past behavior.

Mr. Cattano emphasizes that no cigarette is a safe cigarette and that smoking, regardless of brand, is a definite threat to health.

Whether or not you agree with the theory that most smokers are addicted to nicotine or to the habit of smoking, you may find that you or your friends must use an individual route to giving up cigarettes. A wide variety of schemes has been devised to help those who want to stop, and the support of leaders and fellow sufferers can be obtained for a fee by joining a clinic program. The American Heart Association, the American Cancer Society, or the American Lung Association in your area may help you to locate a nonprofit, inexpensive stop-smoking clinic. All who have studied the problem agree that it is easier not to start than it is to stop smoking, no matter what technique is used.

Can gambling be an addiction? Experts believe that there are between 4 and 10 million people in the United States whose lives are dominated by gambling. Although not everyone agrees, many experts feel that most of these people have a problem of addiction. Certainly, these individuals proceed from occasional to habitual gambling, risking higher and higher stakes. They develop a craving for the pleasurable yet painful tension that accompanies the uncertainty of winning or losing. As compulsive gamblers, they continue their risky activities no matter how self-destructive, compelled by forces over which they have no control. Gambling is irresistible to them, even though material gain is far from certain. Unlike casual gamblers who usually go to the track or casino with friends, compulsive gamblers usually go alone.

Age, social background, education, and other factors vary widely. Dr. Robert L. Custer, a psychiatrist with the Veterans Administration, is an expert on alcohol, drug abuse, and gambling. He suggests the following composite picture of a compulsive gambler in an advance stage: male, age thirty to forty, drinks heavily, sleeps poorly, no financial resources, tense, irritable, has considered suicide, and gambles constantly. The larger percentage of males than females is often considered due to the environment. Then, too, males have greater opportunity to gamble. Dr. Custer suggests that the availability of easy money through a bookie is a factor in the addiction process. He also observes that almost all the gamblers he has treated began gambling when they were adolescents. Opportunity to gamble is only one of the factors involved. Most compulsive gamblers share certain personality characteristics.

Consider the case of Mary. Except for her sex, she has many typical characteristics of problem gamblers. She lives for gambling while neglecting her husband, children, and home. Every cent that she can get goes to the casino with her. She even steals money from her children's piggy banks to gamble, hoping to "make it big." Mary, like other compulsive gamblers, feels important when she is betting. While holding the dice, she feels in control of her world. Through the rituals of gambling, she enjoys an altered state of consciousness, a kind of high that some people obtain from climbing a mountain, walking alone by the ocean's edge, winning a tennis game, or through drug or alcohol use. Mary is not usually a happy person. Her behavior at home is immature and demanding. She is irritable, suffers feelings of unworthiness, helplessness, and inadequacy.

Mary, as most compulsive gamblers, sees herself as a winner. She lives in a dream world in which she is a charming philanthropist. She plans to do wonderful things for her family and friends "when she wins big." Then she hopes to make up for all the problems she has caused by her gambling. Gambling addicts share a desire to have tremendous amounts of material things without making a great effort to obtain them. They maintain a self-image of being all-powerful when gambling, and many say they feel secure only when they are participating in risking their money for big winnings or dreaming about making their betting systems work to bring great luxuries. When they are losing, they continue to gamble, for they feel that they will win everything they have lost if they bet just one more time.

Compulsive gamblers rarely stop betting until they have lost all available money. Then they promise themselves that they will give up their habit. Many individuals go to work, earn enough money to keep themselves and to save thousands of dollars. But then they are tempted to bet some or all of their savings, with the hope that they will win a huge amount. Even though they know that the odds are against them, such gamblers believe they can beat the system and win.

Many people gamble within the limits they set for themselves, and most agree that risk taking is part of everyday living. There is risk involved when one plants seeds in a garden, rides in an automobile, or participates in an almost endless number of activities. But some individuals carry their risk taking to extremes, and will continue to gamble until they have lost all their material possessions.

Gambling is usually defined as betting or wagering, whether or not money is involved. A compulsive gambler bets on all kinds of things, including those in which money is involved. He or she is dominated by the irresistible urge to bet and by an obsessive idea that he or she can win.

Some gamblers realize that their behavior is destructive. They see marriages deteriorating, friends suffering, careers lost, and in many cases they become involved with the law. They rationalize that passing bad checks for cash needed to gamble is just a sort of borrowing since they plan to pay back the money with interest when they make a financial coup. But money that is won usually finds its way back to the gambling scene with the hope that it will bring even more money.

Since money appears to be a major incentive for compulsive gambling, and gamblers cannot manage their finances for everyday living, people ask if the need for money is at the root of the problem. Experts think not. Emotional problems play a much more important part than financial need in this type of addiction.

One man who was imprisoned for gambling read the sports column of a newspaper each morning in jail and picked the likely winners, even though he could not bet on them. Although no money was involved, he waited anxiously each day for the sports results.

The causes of compulsive gambling are not completely understood, though many theories have been offered. Some are extremely complicated and beyond the scope of this book, but there are ideas that may help laypeople in the understanding of the problem. Compulsive gambling has been described as a ritualistic response to anxiety. The compulsive gambler continues to ask, "Is Lady Luck with me?" somewhat the way a child asks a parent, "Do you love me? Do you approve of me?" Since this question can never be satisfactorily answered through gambling, the gambler continues to pose the question and continues to lose until all funds are depleted. Experts say release can be found only by losing.

There is a theory in which compulsive gambling is described as a phase of a high, or manic, reaction; the stage at which all money has been lost is the painful low, or depression, afterward.

According to another theory, the compulsive gambler wants to lose in order to be punished for subconscious thoughts about sex and parents. The wish to lose, of course, is also subconscious. Few dispute the fact that most compulsive gamblers are losers, since even after winning (which is considered to strengthen unconscious guilt feelings), the winnings are used up in an effort to make even larger amounts of money.

Even gamblers who know they cannot win act as if they might. The act of gambling becomes an outlet for stress, and the enjoyment of betting or risk taking, the sense of being important in the action, are more important than the winning or losing of money.

Just as a first drink can lead an alcoholic back to a drunken spree, a first bet can lead a compulsive gambler back to uncontrollable risk taking. In spite of the fact that there may be as many as 10 million compulsive gamblers in the United States, comparatively little research has been done on the subject.

Not only is permanent cure questionable, but many problem gamblers who claim they want to stop would not accept therapy even if it were available. Perhaps one of the reasons that problem gamblers resist treatment is that their symptoms are enjoyable. People who suffer from phobias are more apt to want to relieve their symptoms because their excessive fears are unpleasant. Gambling involves enjoyable feelings, such as the love of conflict, the satisfaction of being an object of jealousy when they are winning, and the pleasure that gamblers derive from using their cunning, concealment, and deceit. The courting of fear adds spice and color to the quality of some gamblers' lives. There is a theory that gambling satisfies certain qualities, such as the need for stimulation and change, that are present in human beings. The fluctuation between self-faith and fear provides a kind of tension that is necessary to life.

The first in-patient program in which professional therapists work with gamblers reports only limited success. Since there appears to be a similarity in the way addictive behavior serves to help both alcoholics and gamblers avoid psychological pain and prevent psychological growth, a treatment program for both kinds of addicts was combined at the Veterans Administration Hospital in Cleveland, Ohio. Dr. Alida Glen, psychologist and program coordinator, believes that both illnesses begin in adolescence, although they have roots in childhood when, in most cases, there appears to have been considerable psychological deprivation. She describes the typical compulsive gambler as appearing to have a personality disorder when first interviewed. The patient shows little remorse for antisocial behavior, offers many rationalizations for it, and is ready to blame others for his/her problems. Other symptoms include being out of touch with one's own feelings, lacking insight, not expecting to be understood, and doubting that she can be helped. Dr. Glen says that if one doubts that gambling can be addictive, interviews with compulsive gamblers can be very revealing.

Many patients who have been treated in the program at Cleveland Veterans Administration Hospital were already members of Gamblers Anonymous. G.A., as it is commonly called, is similar in many ways to Alcoholics Anonymous, or A.A. Today, G.A. has about

450 chapters throughout the United States as well as some in other countries, and it has fostered two offshoots for families of addicts. Gam-Anon is the organization for spouses of compulsive gamblers. Gam-A-Teen sponsors weekly meetings for children of hard-core gamblers, where they help one another to understand their parents' problems.

Gamblers Anonymous began in Los Angeles, California, in 1957 after two compulsive gamblers began leaning on each other for support in controlling their habits. One man, Jim W., had been trying for several years to establish a group of individuals who wanted to overcome gambling problems. After some unsuccessful attempts with others who claimed they wanted to stop, he was discouraged. Then he met Sam, who identified himself as having a problem with gambling. These two men tried with little success to get others to join them, until they were given publicity by Paul Coates. He wrote about them in his newspaper column in the *Los Angeles Mirror* and gave them radio and television time. This column and the TV programs opened the door to those who wanted to share experiences and help each other through such an organization. Today, Gamblers Anonymous has about five-thousand members in the United States alone. Therapeutic talk sessions help some of the members to control their gambling, but many drop out when they relapse into old habits. The cure rate is about 10 percent and the cure is not necessarily permanent.

A combination of Gamblers Anonymous and

therapy such as that offered in the program at Cleveland Veterans Administration Hospital may be more successful in arresting the problem than one alone, but even this is not considered a cure. The therapy program helps patients to think more realistically and to accept support from people who have a different value system. Changing a life-style from one in which gambling is completely dominant is far from easy.

A second in-patient program for compulsive gamblers evolved at the Veterans Administration Hospital in Brooklyn, New York. Under the direction of Dr. Abe S. Kramer, this program involves the same kind of intensive therapy used by Dr. Glen. Patients spend two or three weeks in the hospital, where they are not only isolated from gambling but are helped to cope with the more profound emotional problems that trouble them and which are masked by the gambling addiction. Dr. Kramer, who has treated many compulsive gamblers in private therapy, notes that it is difficult for people to admit that they have a gambling problem. They come to him explaining that they have other problems; the gambling habit is revealed at later sessions.

A new, nonprofit organization, the National Council for Compulsive Gambling, is working toward more funds for research and education. Its founders believe that states that collect revenues from legalized gambling should reserve some of the revenue to publicize the dangers of gambling and pay for research and treatment for the victims.

Efforts are underway to provide treatment at a third hospital, the Veterans Administration Hospital in Palo Alto, California, but treatment facilities are minimal.

While there is no physical withdrawal in overcoming the excessive urge to gamble, some experts believe there may be psychological withdrawal. At this stage, patients suffer from depression and feel guilt-ridden. Support from peers as well as staff members is extremely important at all times. Those in therapy receive support from friends they have made in the program, as well as from successful members of Gamblers Anonymous.

Only a very, very small percentage of people who want help with gambling addictions can take part in hospital therapy programs, even though this approach seems far more helpful than prison. Consider the gambler who went to prison for swindling banks so that he could support his habit. When he was released, he visited seven racetracks in one weekend. Experts agree that prison is no more of a cure for gambling than it is for other addictions.

A person may become a compulsive gambler in as little as six months, although it takes a much longer time for many gamblers to become addicted. How does one know if s/he has a problem? Gamblers who visit offtrack betting parlors in New York City may see a sign that reads, "IS GAMBLING MAKING YOUR LIFE UNHAPPY?" Those who answer this question in the affirmative are directed to dial the number of the National Council on Compulsive Gambling. There they will be invited to attend meetings of Gamblers Anonymous.

According to Gamblers Anonymous, most compulsive gamblers will answer yes to at least seven of the following questions:*

1. Do you lose time from work due to gambling?
2. Is gambling making your home life unhappy?
3. Is gambling affecting your reputation?
4. Have you ever felt remorse after gambling?
5. Do you ever gamble to get money with which to pay debts or to otherwise solve financial difficulties?
6. Does gambling cause a decrease in your ambition or efficiency?
7. After losing do you feel you must return as soon as possible and win back your losses?
8. After a win do you have a strong urge to return and win more?
9. Do you often gamble until your last dollar is gone?
10. Do you ever borrow to finance your gambling?
11. Have you ever sold any real or personal property to finance gambling?
12. Are you reluctant to use "gambling money" for normal expenditures?
13. Does gambling make you careless of the welfare of your family?

*Reprinted through the courtesy of Gamblers Anonymous, National Service Office, P.O. Box 17173, Los Angeles, Calif., 90017.

14. Do you ever gamble longer than you planned?
15. Do you ever gamble to escape worry or trouble?
16. Have you ever committed, or considered committing, an illegal act to finance gambling?
17. Does gambling cause you to have difficulty sleeping?
18. Do arguments, disappointments, or frustrations create within you an urge to gamble?
19. Do you have an urge to celebrate any good fortune by a few hours of gambling?
20. Have you ever considered self-destruction as a result of your gambling?

No one knows the exact number of people who would answer seven of these questions in the affirmative. Professor Tomas Martinez, a University of Colorado sociologist, claims that a gambling epidemic is present in the United States now, but it may take many years before the government recognizes this. Until it does, research about compulsive gamblers will continue to be very limited.

Will the number of compulsive gamblers increase with the growing number of states in which gambling is being legalized? No one really knows the answer to this question. Some experts believe that people who will become compulsive gamblers already have the ample opportunity to do so and more legalized gambling will not cause additional problems. Others believe that any round-the-clock gambling casinos could well play a part in the shift of some gamblers from casual to compulsive. Since adolescence is the period in which many compulsive gamblers begin their pattern of addiction, some sociologists and psychologists recommend that no one under twenty-one be permitted to participate in legalized gambling. Experts would also encourage education to inform the public of the risks as well as the pleasures of gambling.

Considering the number of people who already have a serious problem with gambling and considering the growth of gambling, whether or not it is legalized, the need for more research is overwhelming. The research by Professor Tomas Martinez is a step in the right direction.

Professor Martinez has spent many years studying gambling. After completing a two-year general study, he concentrated on fifty people who seemed to gamble compulsively. In his research over a four-year period, Professor Martinez spent more than two-hundred hours playing games of chance such as roulette, dice, card games, horse racing, keno, and bingo. He played in six commercial card parlors where gambling is legal and made twenty-five visits to casinos in Nevada. He also attended weekly meetings of Gamblers Anonymous for a period of seven months as an observer. During this time, he made some casual friendships with compulsive gamblers. About a dozen members visited Professor Martinez at his home, and about twenty-five regular and occasional members of Gamblers Anonymous provided taped interviews.

Among the areas explored extensively in Professor

Martinez's research was the examination of five major conscious moods that a person undergoes in becoming a compulsive gambler. The first of these moods, risk taking, is considered by some experts to be the essence of gambling. When a gambler is engaged in risk taking, s/he feels filled with life. The second conscious mood is called "here and now" and means that the mind's full attention is on the situation at hand. Such a mind is free from other matters and is a pleasant experience for gamblers. Some gamblers have described this mood by saying, "Once I get into it, then I can relax." Another common expression used to describe this mood is "I close off the world outside when I sit down at the gambling table." Feeling "alive" when in action is another common expression.

As a gambler becomes more deeply involved, part of the mind becomes free to fantasize. This is the third conscious mood. Dreams are luxurious and the person experiences a sense of high self-esteem. This sense of power, which is imagined, seems real to the gambler. Professor Martinez found that there were three types of fantasies for gamblers in this third conscious mood. One type mentally reconstructs a past situation but puts him/herself in a more glamorous or more favorable light. As a member of the cast in the recalled event, the gambler plays the part with special learned abilities or has the advantage of hindsight. The personal biography is rewritten so that in the fantasy the gambler feels a sense of high self-esteem. For example, the person might recall a situation in high school in which s/he outwitted rivals in various situations even though this was not the case. In the second type of fantasy, the gambler imagines him/herself at the present time as a prestigious and important person who is performing daring actions. One gambler who took part in the research imagined himself as an international gambler with international money backing him. In the third type of fantasy the gambler visualizes a future in which luck brings large amounts of money and enables him/her to be a philanthropist on a grand scale. Mary's fantasy, mentioned earlier in this chapter, is an example.

In the fourth conscious mood, euphoria is experienced. This is the high mentioned earlier. It is this state, along with fantasy, that the research indicated must occur as the person passes from an occasional to compulsive gambler. And these moods help to create the social conditions that make possible the fifth conscious mood, that of mysticism. For the ritualistic meaning, there must be a large investment of self. In this mood, the gambler feels omnipotent. When a gambler reaches this stage, money is valuable only to keep the player in the action of gambling. Enhancing pleasure is more important than winning, and the gambler will stay in action until all is lost. Then s/he will rush around to get more money so that it is possible to get back in the action.

Quitting while ahead is almost always impossible for the compulsive gambler, so it is obvious that such a gambler is a loser. When losses arc so great that they interfere with the power to dream, gamblers become dissatisfied and awaken from the dreamlike existence they have led. Now they experience self-hate, and resolutions to quit gambling are made. These are not kept because self-deception is common, with the gambler believing that s/he can "take it or leave it" much the way many alcoholics and other drug addicts deceive themselves at a similar stage.

It is at this point, says Professor Martinez, that the compulsive gambler finds it easier to give in to the desire to gamble than to fight it—even though there is a negative self-evaluation developing. Unpleasant events have invaded the scene, but the completion of the act of losing all gambling resources is the mechanism that produces relief from tension. So gambling continues until the person hits rock bottom. Professor Martinez characterizes *rock bottom* as a state in which one or more of the following conditions are present: loss of job, loss of family, prison sentence from bad checks or other financial maneuvering to gain money for gambling, a suicidal personality. At rock bottom, the introduction of new behavior patterns become possible. The gambler now can accept the fact that former behavior was self-defeating. Unfortunately, most compulsive gamblers are loners, and when they reach this stage, they do not seek help from others easily. They are depressed, but they feel that other people would not understand what they have done. The dream world no longer exists. Now it is a painful world.

In his research Professor Martinez has shown the development of a compulsive gambler from one perspective; other researchers may look at the compulsive gambler through different eyes. Research studies may be valuable not only for the understanding of how one develops from a casual to a compulsive gambler but may help to show how other addictions develop.

Dr. Robert Custer of the Veterans Administration has researched compulsive gambling in a wide variety of areas. The problems of compulsive women gamblers is one of them. Only about 5 percent of the members of Gamblers Anonymous are women, but this is probably not an accurate reflection of the total number. There may be many women who hide their problems from friends and neighbors, and even from a group such as Gamblers Anonymous where their problems would be confidential. Dr. Custer compares women compulsive gamblers today to women alcoholics of ten years ago. One study, by the Survey Research Center of the Institute for Social Research at the University of Michigan, estimated that there were nearly half as many women compulsive gamblers as men. This is a great many women.

Dr. Custer believes that women develop their gambling problems in a somewhat different way from men, but both end with the same tangle of lies and debts. Women usually learn gambling from fathers, male companions, or husbands, whereas men usually learn at an earlier age from peers. Women start at a later age and don't become reckless as fast; they are considered good players. Many compulsive women gamblers are housewives who are extremely good at juggling debts from credit cards and from finance companies. Just as their male counterparts do, women compulsive gamblers come from all walks of life. In his research, Dr. Custer found that many women seemed to have been suffering from a mild depression before they began to gamble for excitement and attention.

While Gamblers Anonymous does provide a tremendous amount of help for both female and male compulsive gamblers, there may be millions of people who never contact such a group or who need additional kinds of help.

As you can see from reading this chapter, treatment of compulsive gambling is not very successful. Therefore, as in the case of some other types of addiction, emphasis on prevention is especially important. Certainly gambling is an area in which far more research is needed both in the areas of prevention and treatment.

The only voluntary health agency in the United States established to combat the disease of compulsive gambling is the National Council on Compulsive Gambling. This council was incorporated in 1975 to disseminate information and provide education on compulsive gambling as an illness and a public-health problem. It seeks to stimulate the concern of the medical profession, educators, legislators, and the criminal-justice system in the nationwide problem of gambling by supplying community services and medical treatment for compulsive gamblers and their families.

In addition to referring gamblers to Gamblers Anonymous, the most successful program to date for the compulsive gambler, many families are referred to Gam-Anon and Gam-A-Teen which are outgrowths of Gamblers Anonymous. But thousands of compulsive gamblers still languish in prison and mental institutions and many live in disrupted family situations.

The National Council on Compulsive Gambling proposes a program aimed at the reduction and prevention of compulsive gambling by mobilizing public support through local and professional groups.

ADDICTION TO FOOD 4

BY ALICE D. OUTWATER,
Counselor/Therapist at the University of Vermont
Counseling and Testing Center. Mrs. Outwater
has a longstanding interest in overweight
and runs diet groups for students and faculty
with a three-pronged approach of nutrition, exercise,
and counseling with a retraining of eating habits.

Might you become a food addict? Few people want to be fat, yet approximately 10 percent to 40 percent of school-age children are overweight, and this proportion is steadily rising. Since 50 percent to 85 percent of overweight children remain obese as adults, there is an urgent need to understand and help young people do something about this problem. In some segments of the American population, obesity is so common one might say it has reached epidemic proportions!

There was a time when excess weight was considered a sign of prosperity and abundance. Plumpness spoke well for a person, for it indicated a comfortable position in life. Today we know better. We know that a fat person is not necessarily well nourished and that the added pounds may lead to serious health problems. Excessive body weight puts an undue strain on the heart, and in the predisposed individuals, it encourages the emergence of latent diabetes. Obesity also increases the liability to diseases such as high blood pressure and hardening of the arteries. It is associated with respiratory, liver, and gall-bladder disease, as well as osteoarthritis (from the pressure of excess pounds on the weight-bearing joints), varicose veins, and a host of other conditions that can subtract years from a normal life span. These diseases are far more common in obese persons and sometimes lead to sudden death. Although not all obese persons will encounter these health problems, it is well known that excessive weight can aggravate existing disorders and cause more pronounced symptoms, or that the disorders may appear at an earlier age than would be expected in a person of normal weight. For example, diabetes is four times more common in obese individuals, and the risk of high blood pressure is twice as great, as is the possibility of cerebral hemorrhage. When these people reach their normal weight, their diseases often become less serious and the symptoms minimal; high blood pressure may be considerably reduced or even level off to a normal range. A well-planned diet program can do much to minimize the risks and to increase the likelihood of a longer, more comfortable life.

The drives for food and activity are regulated by mechanisms that are extremely complex. For some people overeating and being big seem to be a necessary adjustment in the handling of their lives—it is an adaptation that appears to be best for them. Perhaps these people are "normal for themselves" when overweight. Still others reduce and stay thin but cannot relax, as they are constantly preoccupied with their weight. So these people, known as the "thin fat people," keep themselves in a state of tension. No matter how slim they are, they still consider themselves overweight and seem to have the same adjustment problems as their obese counterparts.

Obesity is rarely associated with a brain tumor, although in earlier times it was fashionable to cite this as a cause. This condition is so rare that a physician will seldom see a case in a lifetime of general practice. A possible cause of obesity is an imbalance or slowing down of the metabolism. Some individuals have a normal food intake and good exercise patterns, yet remain obese.

Research usually does not focus on one single measurement to tell the complete story of obesity but rather considers a fuller picture of how disturbances in carbohydrate metabolism, glandular function, growth processes, and other regulatory mechanisms combine to produce the complex syndrome of obesity.

What does it mean to be overweight or obese? Almost everyone who is more than 20 percent overweight is also overfat or obese. Obesity is a state of having more adipose tissue (fat) than is consistent with the body build. However, not all heavy people are excessively fat. You must take into account that bone (body build) and muscle vary from person to person, and recognizing these differences can be difficult. This is why most weight charts are divided into three classifications of skeletal size—small, medium, and large frame—often giving a twenty-pound range of acceptable weight for the height.

Another consideration in judging obesity is the amount of excess body fat on the person. A boy on the football team, working out daily, may be twenty-five pounds heavier than a sedentary classmate of the same height. The athletic boy's weight may be largely in muscle, while the sedentary boy's is in fat. The latter then might be considered excessively overweight. A simple way of assessing body fatness is to measure the size of the triceps skinfold, which is the subcutaneous fat deposit over the triceps muscle on the back of the upper arm.

Recently scientists have learned much about the "organ" of obesity—adipose (fatty) tissue. It appears that in the adult there are normally a fixed number of fat cells, and this number varies with the individual. Think of them as tiny balloons that can be inflated or deflated according to need. They increase in size as they store excess fat and decrease in size as existing fat stores are used up. These lipocytes, as they are called scientifically, vary in their fat content during a lifetime but never diminish in number.

The total number of fat cells in the body is fixed by mid-to-late teens. During infancy, overfeeding with rapid weight gain can cause these fat cells to increase to two to five times normal in the still developing adipose tissues. These cells will not decrease in later life once they are established, despite weight-reduction efforts. It also becomes considerably more difficult for these people to lose weight.

Who is a food addict? It is not clear whether all obese people should be considered food addicts. The compulsive person who eats to the detrimental effect of his health and who thinks about food to an unusual degree might qualify. Some excessive eaters seem compulsively driven by inner forces that they can neither understand nor control. This is apparently not because of taste or hunger, as they often stuff themselves without enjoyment to the point of illness. Of course, not all overeaters or grossly obese persons are compulsive eaters or food addicts. There may be other physiological (metabolic or—rarely—genetic), socio-cultural, and psychological factors interreacting as well.

Obesity is considered less destructive than alcohol or drug dependence, but it seriously affects and undermines the well-being of a person as well as his/her domestic and interpersonal relationships. The overweight are often discriminated against in finding employment, and ridiculed by others in society. They may feel unattractive and unloved, become depressed and miserable, and tend to withdraw from social contacts, becoming ever more isolated and lonely. Fortunately, none of the antisocial activities that occur with alcohol, drugs, and gambling follow in the wake of this.

However obesity is defined, there is now general

agreement that persistence in overeating can serve as a substitute for other satisfactions, especially emotional ones, and it is looked upon with seriousness.

Relief eating usually shows up in an inadequate or anxious personality who wants to complement his regular food intake when feeling in need of a comforter during depression, tension, anger, loneliness, or boredom. However, the "eating binge" may increase guilt feelings, which leads to more eating as the anxiety increases. This requires even further relief overeating.

It is then that these compulsive or relief eaters begin to look for the "magic solution" in crash diets or pills (amphetamines) that promise quick weight loss. This seems to be an easier solution than following a sensible diet that would take more time. They do lose a few pounds rapidly, but then quickly gain them back, often with more to spare. People have been known to gain and lose over a hundred pounds a year this way, while unable to hold the weight loss. The body is put through trauma trying to adjust and would be better off with the weight left on. Workers in the health field agree to the importance of eating wisely, while following a well-balanced diet. Gradual weight loss over a longer period of time has a better chance of being held. This will avoid the nervousness, irritability, weakness, and loss of skin and muscle tone that too rapid weight loss triggers.

Fasting existed in prehistoric cultures, and is still practiced among many primitive peoples. In some religions and cultures particular times are often set aside for fasting. In modern times, Mahatma Gandhi of India fasted for community benefit in protest against violent excesses. A host of religions, including the Roman Catholic and Jewish faiths, observe certain fast days. A number of popular books have come out on fasting as a means of losing weight. However, this method must be approached with utmost caution, and only under a doctor's supervision, as fasting over a period of time without liquids may be disastrous. For teenagers, at a time when the body is undergoing many changes, any fasting can be a very dangerous thing to do.

Severe restriction of calories forces the body to use its stores of glycogen; then other tissues in addition to the fatty ones are drawn upon to supply energy needs. This can have undesirable effects. When there is inadequate protein in the body, sufficient amino acids for the body's enzyme systems may not be supplied. Amino acids are building blocks for many other nutrients. Imbalances can interfere with absorption and increase needs for other amino acids, thus affecting growth and repair of tissues.

As the whole metabolism of the body is intricately balanced, interfering with one aspect of it may start a chain reaction and disrupt the entire system. Too rapid weight loss can upset the hormone balance and cause menstruation to cease among girls. Normal bodily development and growth may be retarded in other ways. Hair can become thin and begin to fall out and skin tone become blotchy and unhealthy.

Anorexia nervosa, a condition that results in starving the body, has become increasingly prevalent among teenagers, especially girls. Some young people may decide to diet and lose weight, but as they reach goal weight, all sense of perspective vanishes and they continue dieting with fanatic zeal until their weight drops into a danger zone. These people are literally starving themselves to death. Then hospitalization becomes necessary and the patients must be sustained on intravenous feedings in an attempt to reverse the body metabolism. If this reversal does not take place, death is certain.

Sometimes young people decide they have eaten too much and make themselves vomit after a meal. This can rapidly become habit forming. As they continue eating binges followed by bouts of self-inflicted vomiting, their weight can drop drastically, their eyes have dark circles, and their overall appearance can become gaunt. A picture of such a person shows the rib cage protruding and a ghastly appearance. In spite of these signs, people who suffer from this addiction continue to see themselves in the mirror as too fat, so they put their bodies through further weight loss. This may lead to more hospitalization, and even long-term work with a psychologist or psychiatrist may be needed to break the habit.

An intelligent approach to dieting would be to decrease the quantity of normal foods eaten (for instance, cutting out all junk foods might be quite effective). A reduction of 500 calories a day will probably assure a good weight loss at the steady rate of one or two pounds a week. Be sure that you have included the four basic food groups: (1) milk; (2) meat, poultry, and fish; (3) fruits and vegetables; (4) bread and cereal every day to assure a balanced diet. This will also help retrain faulty eating habits, and should be fairly easy to maintain over a lifetime.

Everyone knows of the "sweet tooth" obese people often have, and this desire for sweets can add calories and pounds to their bodies. There has been a steady rise in sugar consumption over the past 150 years as the demand and availability increase. But many researchers feel the addictive effect of sugar consists in the addiction to a sweet taste, not to sugar itself. This taste apparently can be supplied by substitutes, as dieters know. They can become accustomed to using sweeteners instead of sugar. However, the researchers do point out the actual addictiveness to sugar at this point is "not proven."

Recently baby-food manufacturers have begun to eliminate or reduce the added sugar in over one-hundred products in their baby-food lines. Critics have charged that the extras such as sugar, salt, and artificial colorings are inserted to make the products more appealing to grown-ups! The infants are indifferent to these "improved" colors and tastes, and some researchers feel they may have harmful side effects. It is suspected that sugar leads to tooth decay, obesity, and perhaps other common ills.

Does temperament have anything to do with obesity? Some researchers have observed in many cases that a sluggish temperament and the tendency to be inactive preceded the beginning of obesity, and that the existence of obesity only reinforced these conditions. Hilda Bruch, M.D., of Baylor University in Texas observed that children who were rated as most inactive also had the highest food intake and were most disturbed emotionally. Others would agree that fat children seen on a playground moved and ran about far less than their slimmer classmates. It would appear important to urge overweight young people to increase their activity level and have them engage in some type of regular exercise.

What makes people overeat? In a study of 115 obese adolescent girls, the majority went on eating sprees when they felt tense, nervous, depressed, bored, worried, etc. Dr. Bruch feels that people who do this seem to suffer from an inability to identify their bodily sensations correctly—in particular, hunger and satiation. She hypothesizes that this occurs as the result of disturbed early mother-child interactions in which the mother would repeatedly feed the child inappropriately when s/he was not hungry—so that the child never learned to identify the stimuli arising from his own stomach. The statement "I don't know when I'm hungry" points to a lack of basic trust in one's own feelings and the inability to identify these feelings.

Learning experiences are registered in the brain. When there are appropriate responses the child will be able to correctly identify his/her experiences and other sensations, thoughts, and feelings. As the child grows into adulthood, regardless of difficulties encountered, s/he will be essentially self-directed in experiences, able to make good judgments and willing to act upon them. Adults who never learned as children to identify the amount of food their body needs will continue to misjudge this. They will overeat to the point of stuffing, without consciously realizing it.

Albert J. Stunkard, M.D., and Myer Mendelson, M.D., psychiatrists at the University of Pennsylvania, propose that obesity is the only condition that involves at the same time a disturbance in body image and a disturbance in impulse control. Many obese people are revolted by the sight of their bodies and rarely look in the mirror; some even avoid shopping for fear of seeing themselves in store windows. Others become so self-conscious that they misconceive how they are viewed, blaming everything bad that happens to them on their weight. Many are uncomfortable with the opposite sex and either avoid or actively dislike them. Drs. Stunkard and Mendelson followed a group of children for thirty years and found the odds against an obese child becoming a normal-weight adult were

4 to 1; for those who did not reduce during adolescence, it was more than 28 to 1.

To understand the psychological causes of eating one must look at our American culture and habits. Food is important from the early years, not only as nourishment but sometimes as a substitute for love and affection. A child from toddler age on is rewarded with cookies and candies, lollipops and ice cream cones. Festive occasions center on eating; holidays that entail family gatherings, such as Thanksgiving, include rich foods of all kinds.

People spend increasingly large amounts of time in front of the TV, where a majority of the commercials have to do with food or preparation of food—usually rich and calorie filled. Try to get an apple or orange for dessert at any of our fast-food chains!

Eating habits may be set before we are out of the cradle. Some of us are already overeating and have unconsciously acquired tastes and habits that may eventually lead to overweight when we reach adolescence. Henry A. Jordan, M.D., and Leonard S. Levitz, Ph.D., both in the department of psychiatry at the University of Pennsylvania, cite the example of the baby who is breast-fed when s/he is born. The baby sucks until satisfied, and the mother does not know how much milk the baby has consumed. But her baby seems content and, one might say, taking care of his/her own needs. Physiologically, the mother produces milk according to the child's demands. When the child is put on the bottle, the mother has a visual clue and can see how much the child has consumed. She may now tend to shape the child's eating behavior according to her own attitudes about how much the child should eat. Now it becomes possible for her to over- or underfeed the child. The parent, without realizing it, assumes a greater role in teaching, shaping, and modeling the feeding behavior. If she is from a cultural background where eating a large amount is synonymous with health, she will urge her baby to eat more, and "stuff." Here the pattern has been set for eating more calories than the body actually requires, and the number of fat cells will increase.

Overweight is a result of excessive eating or of eating more food than the body uses for energy. Morton B. Glenn, M.D., past president of the American College of Nutrition, says that 90 percent of overweight people are fast eaters. The majority are stand-up eaters, people who do more eating while standing than when sitting. And did you know that many overweight people are such plate-cleaners that when they are through eating, their dishes look washed?

Tension can be a strong factor in overeating. Our days have tension of varying degrees and duration. It can include such everyday concerns as "Will I be called on in class when I'm not prepared?" or "Will I be asked to the dance next week?" or "What will my father do if he doesn't find a job?" Some are within our control, some are not; and many of us feel like a mass of tangled tensions, one superimposed on another.

Many people respond by eating. Thin individuals may respond by loss of appetite, but people who tend to be overweight often find some comfort in eating. They may not actually be hungry; but the tensions build up and from habit they deal with it by eating, even stuffing themselves.

What other alternatives do you have? If you recognize the above behavior as yours, you might try the following route. You may have been on numerous fad diets for short periods of time and often lost a few pounds. Probably you have always gained them back, plus a few more. When you approach dieting in a sensible and long-lasting way it is hard work. You must first change your eating habits and go on a nutritionally balanced diet. This would include ample carbohydrates, fats, and proteins. Write down everything you eat for a week—breakfast, lunch, and dinner, plus all snacks. You may be surprised at the number of junk foods you have been indulging in, especially if you run to the snack bar or refrigerator whenever you feel uneasy.

Study your record carefully and look for weak spots. Check a height-weight chart to see how many calories you should eat to maintain your present weight; reduce it by 500 calories. This should help you lose a pound or two each week, and extra exercise will increase the weight loss. The exercise will also help you firm up your body as the pounds begin to drop off; it will make you feel less hungry if done before meals. Walking, jogging, bicycling, and jumping rope are among the easiest ways to exercise and are very beneficial to the system. Doing any one of these regularly will also make the dieting easier.

If you want psychological support, gather together a group of ove weight friends to join in a project. After a physical examination to rule out any health problems, you can proceed. Have each person set a goal weight according to his/her height and body build. There will be discouraging times when you go off the diet, but treat each day as a new beginning. Over a period of several months, losing about two pounds a week, you will gradually reach your goal. You should find yourself with more energy and be able to tackle tasks that may have been a problem before. As you begin to lose weight, you may need to get used to your new body image. It can be exciting but sometimes strange not worrying about being fat and wondering what clothes will fit you!

If you approach your weight problem as a personal responsibility and a task to be handled in a systematic way, you will begin to understand it. By writing down everything you eat and calculating the calorie amounts, you will become aware of how much your past overeating has been a habit. Now you can put yourself in control of the situation.

In order to maintain your goal weight, you may have to view it as a lifetime commitment, and always be careful about your eating. Weigh yourself weekly to be sure you haven't gained, and if you have go right back on the diet.

Food addiction and overweight are problems common to many adolescents and are immensely complex, but there are many approaches that can be considered to tackle them. Understanding yourself and your food habits is primary; then deciding to do something, and going about it patiently and systematically, is probably your best solution.

When coffee prices began to rise in recent years, some people reacted by switching to tea, while others refused to give up their coffee no matter what the financial cost. Relatively few considered whether they were addicted to the caffeine in coffee and tea. Cola drinkers tend to select their favorite brand, and those who drink several glasses a day complain when they cannot obtain it. Here, too, caffeine addiction plays a part.

While withdrawal effects from lack of caffeine are not severe, headaches and irritability are common complaints when caffeine addicts go without their usual supply. Others complain of depression, which is not surprising. The action of caffeine on the central nervous system is that of a stimulant. In controlled experiments, the caffeine found in several cups of coffee enabled participants to have a greater sustained intellectual effort and a keener appreciation of sensory stimuli. Drowsiness and fatigue were diminished and there was a clearer and more rapid flow of thought. Typists have been tested after coffee drinking and shown that they could work faster with fewer errors under very special testing conditions. But many people react in the opposite way. If a person has recently learned a motor skill that involves accurate timing and delicate muscular coordination, there may be a decrease in efficiency.

The number of cups of coffee consumed in the United States every year has been estimated as 160 billion cups, or roughly 740 cups per person. Since there are many non-coffee drinkers, the number of cups for those who do drink coffee is higher by far. Measured in pounds, the annual consumption per person in the United States is estimated at 17 pounds. Tea consumption is increasing in the United States as coffee consumption decreases. In England, where tea consumption is already very high, estimates of 10 pounds of tea per person appear reasonably accurate. Both coffee and tea drinkers often say that they could not make it through the day without their favorite beverage.

Cola is popular over a wide age range. Recently a panel of Food and Drug Administration advisers disagreed about the potential health hazard of cola drinks, especially for children. The principal concern of those who felt the drinks unsafe was the exposure of children to caffeine in a period of growth and brain development. A cola drink of the twelve-ounce size contains about two-thirds the amount of caffeine found in a cup of coffee. Many people drink no colas, but others drink many each day. Each person in the

United States averages the daily consumption of caffeine from cola drinks that is equal to the caffeine in about a quarter cup of coffee. If this amount were spread equally among all the people, there would be little cause for alarm. But just as there are coffee and tea addicts, there are people who are addicted to colas. Many children as young as two are given colas by their parents, so this habit can begin early in life.

Another source of caffeine is cocoa, which contains more per cup than an equal amount of cola but less than coffee. Researchers at the Addiction Research Foundation of Ontario, Canada, estimate that cola drinks have about 40 milligrams of caffeine per serving and that a small chocolate bar has about 25 milligrams. If a 60-pound (27-kilogram) child drinks three colas per day, the child would consume 7.2 milligrams of caffeine per kilogram of weight. That is the equivalent of a 175-pound person drinking eight cups of coffee per day. And one must consider that the child may also eat several chocolate bars on a day when several colas are drunk.

An adult coffee or tea drinker may have difficulty estimating the amount of caffeine taken daily because of milk or cream that is added. And the strength of coffee and tea varies from cup to cup and with personal taste.

Comparing the amount of caffeine in various beverages is difficult too. Estimates of the amount of caffeine in six-ounce portions follow: coffee—70 to 150 milligrams; tea—36 to 100 milligrams; cocoa—50 mil-

ligrams; cola drinks—20 to 30 milligrams. Decaffeinated coffee has most of the caffeine removed; it is estimated that 33 cups of decaffeinated coffee equals the
caffeine level of one cup of regular coffee. Ounce for
ounce, coffee contains more caffeine than tea, cocoa,
and colas.

Caffeine is a drug in a group of chemicals called
xanthines, which are central nervous system stimulants. Caffeine is usually not the only xanthine in the
common beverages that is a stimulant. While all the
xanthines have the same general effect on the body,
they do so in different degrees. Theophylline and
theobromine are two methylxanthines that act with
caffeine in affecting such things as involuntary muscles, voluntary muscles, heart action, kidneys, and the
central nervous system. Since they excite the cerebral
cortex of the brain, which is responsible for sensory
awareness, motor function, and many other functions,
it is not surprising that people claim they can think
more clearly and that they are more aware after drinking a beverage that contains caffeine and other xanthines.

How addictive are caffeine and these related compounds? Reactions vary. For some individuals, daily
intake of small amounts of caffeine can lead to mild
emotional dependence. Many individuals develop
physical dependence from the consumption of five or
more cups of coffee a day. An appreciable degree of
tolerance may develop to some effects of the caffeine.

According to legend, the effect of coffee on the

human body was first noted about A.D. 850 when an Arabian goatherd was perplexed by the unusual activity of his flock. He ate some of the same berries from the bush on which the goats were feeding and he experienced the stimulating effect. This has been called the world's first coffee break.

Many more recent experiments have confirmed the stimulating and the addictive nature of coffee and other caffeine beverages. Drs. Avram Goldstein and Sophia Kaizer of the Department of Pharmacology of the Stanford University School of Medicine performed a classic study that helped to answer questions about whether or not coffee is addictive. They first questioned 289 wives in a housing unit for married graduate students. Of these, 45 percent answered that their coffee drinking was a habit, 31 percent said they felt the need for it, and 42 percent said that it got them going in the morning. Of the moderate and heavy coffee drinkers (those who drank more than three cups per day) there was evidence of withdrawal symptoms if they missed their morning coffee. These women described themselves as irritable, suffering from headache, inability to work effectively, nervousness, restlessness, and sometimes lethargy. These were subjective observations, difficult to evaluate accurately, so this part of the experiment led to a more carefully controlled experiment.

In a double-blind experiment, one in which neither the researchers nor the participants knew the amount of caffeine involved, the effect of coffee on the human body was well demonstrated. The subjects were 18 non-coffee-drinking women and 38 women who drank at least five cups a day. Each participant was given 9 coded glass vials containing specially prepared instant coffee. One vial was used each morning to prepare the breakfast or prebreakfast cup of coffee. For each individual, 3 vials contained coffee with 300 milligrams of caffeine, the equivalent of two or three cups of coffee; 3 vials contained coffee with 150 milligrams of caffeine; and 3 had coffee with no caffeine. Before drinking their morning coffee, the women recorded their moods. They repeated this recording of moods every thirty minutes for the next two hours.

Computerized results confirmed the responses of the earlier experiment in which women responded to questions about coffee drinking and feelings. The heavy coffee drinkers reported that they felt less alert, more sleepy, and more irritable before their morning coffee. On days when these women had coffee in which there was no caffeine, they continued to feel that way even though they were not aware of its absence. Withdrawal symptoms were not present on days in which they had coffee from vials that included caffeine. The non-coffee drinkers reported nervousness and other unpleasant stimuli effects on days when they drank morning coffee made from the vials that contained caffeine. They also reported some gastrointestinal disturbances on those same days.

Many coffee drinkers report that they do not need the results of experiments to convince them that coffee is an addictive stimulant. Since some researchers feel that there are unpleasant side effects for heavy coffee drinkers, they suggest that people drink decaffeinated coffee. One approach to drinking less caffeine without suffering withdrawal symptoms is suggested by Professor Lynn T. Kozlowski, at Wesleyan University in Connecticut. This psychologist suggests mixing decaffeinated coffee with regular coffee to avoid needless overdosing with caffeine.

Caffeine is a poison that can kill if taken in large enough doses, but the fatal dose would be very difficult to ingest by drinking coffee. It would mean drinking from seventy to one-hundred cups of coffee in a short period of time in order to obtain the ten grams, the amount considered fatal. While such huge amounts of caffeine are rarely, if ever, taken at one time, people have been known to become quite ill from drinking too much coffee and from taking too many pills that contain caffeine. One gram of caffeine, the amount in about ten cups of coffee, has been known to produce such "coffee nerves" that insomnia, restlessness, and excitement progressed to mild delirium.

Coffee addicts, tea addicts, and people who overdose on colas, chocolate bars, and cocoa suffer from a syndrome known as *caffeinism*. Chronic high doses of caffeine may produce symptoms so severe that they are confused with *anxiety neurosis*. In one case, a doctor was treating a prisoner with tranquilizers for severe anxiety until he discovered that the man was drinking almost fifty cups of coffee each day. When he reduced his coffee consumption to about twenty cups, the symptoms vanished, even though this amount is still extremely large.

While high doses of caffeine are obviously harmful, the case against lower doses has not been proven. Moderate amounts, while possibly addictive, may well be beneficial to people who have no health problems. For those who have difficulty in restricting the amount of coffee and tea drinking, mixing decaffeinated coffee with regular coffee, either in a coffee maker or by alternating drinks, can help. Weaker coffee and tea also reduce the amount of caffeine. Much depends on how one tolerates this popular and legal stimulant.

Dr. Frederick Evans of the University of Pennsylvania has suggested that naps might be superior to coffee breaks as afternoon stimulants. For some of the people he tested, brief naps provided definite psychological and physical benefits. Participants were better able to solve complex math problems and felt less anxious and stressful after the brief naps. For many who have overcome caffeine addictions, the nap habit may be a welcome form of stimulation.

Cocaine is a drug extracted from the dried leaves of the coca plant, *Erythroxlyon coca*. This shrub is very different from *cocoa*, (or *cacao*) the plant that produces chocolate. Coca has been cultivated for thousands of years in the warm areas of the Andes Mountains in South America, where the leaves are chewed by as much as 90 percent of the adult male population. Workers in Bolivia, Peru, and some other countries of South America use the coca leaves to maintain their strength where oxygen supply is reduced in the highlands; there nonacclimated strangers become exhausted from the slightest physical exertion. This use of cocaine does not appear to be addictive, since the workers who move to lower altitudes after their productive years are said to abandon the use easily.

Cocaine is only one of the active chemicals known as alkaloids that are present in coca leaves, and South American Indians are reported to prefer leaves with a low cocaine content. This may be due to the fact that there are other desirable substances present.

When coca was introduced into Europe in the middle of the nineteenth century, various drinks were made from its leaves. One, known as Mariani's wine, was very popular among artists and religious men. It helped the latter withstand the pangs of hunger during prolonged fasts, and some experts suggest it may have caused visions. In 1885, a patent medicine with similar ingredients was introduced in the United States under the name French Wine Coca. During the following year, the same manufacturer introduced a syrup as a patent medicine made from coca and kola nuts with the now internationally famous name of Coca-Cola. The coca supplied cocaine and the kola nuts supplied caffeine. Both supplied flavor. At the time it was introduced, Coca-Cola was claimed to relieve a long list of ailments.

Pressure to remove cocaine from the coca leaves used in medications and other products resulted in laws forbidding such use. By the time these laws were passed, the cocaine had been removed from the coca leaves used to make Coca-Cola, and it had become a popular beverage rather than a patent medicine. Today the cocaine is removed from the leaves, which still help to provide flavor, and the kola provides some flavor and some stimulation in the form of caffeine (as mentioned in Chapter 5).

Cocaine in pure form had been isolated from the

coca leaf as early as 1844, but it did not become well known until 1883, when a German army physician experimented with it on a group of soldiers during maneuvers. He reported the beneficial fatigue-reducing effects in an article that came to the attention of Sigmund Freud. At that time, Dr. Freud was suffering from depression, chronic fatigue, and other problems. He tested small amounts on himself and supplied some of the drugs to friends, colleagues, and his future wife, Martha. Based on his own reaction, Freud thought of cocaine as a "magical drug," but his opinion changed at a later date when he recognized its dangerous properties.

One of the people to whom Dr. Freud gave cocaine was Dr. Ernst von Fleischl-Marxow, a patient who was suffering from excruciating pain due to a medical problem. At first, the cocaine was a welcome substitute for the morphine to which he had become addicted, but Dr. Fleischl had to gradually increase the doses of cocaine to achieve the same effect. In other words, tolerance to cocaine had developed. It was so great that after a year he was taking a full gram each day. This was many times the dose Freud took from time to time. The cost of Dr. Fleischl's supply of cocaine was enormous by the standards of his day, but the fact that his increased use of cocaine led to a characteristic psychosis was even worse. In this illness the patient believes that insects or snakes are crawling along the skin or under it. Dr. Fleischl suffered tremendously, even though Dr. Freud and other physician friends faithfully nursed him through long and difficult nights.

Why was Freud able to use cocaine on an occasional basis without becoming addicted? Was this because he did not use the drug regularly? It has been suggested that there are important biochemical differences between people who do not become addicted to cocaine and those who do. It has also been suggested that there was a personality difference between these two men. There may be such a difference between people who become addicted and those who do not. However, while it is said that Freud did not have an addictive personality, his addiction to cigars is described in the three-volume biography of him by Dr. Ernest Jones.*

Cocaine's addictive properties are the subject of much discussion, especially now that it has become socially popular among users who can afford it, or who think it is worth the high price. There is limited scientific information about the hazards of "social" use in the medical literature. One writer claims that doctors know so little about cocaine that there is danger in their not understanding the proper treatment if a patient receives a medical overdose when it is used as an anesthetic.

Few doctors will see those who overdose on illegal cocaine, for two reasons. One is the speed with which

---

*Ernest Jones *The Life and Work of Sigmund Freud,* 3 vols. (New York: Basic Books, 1953).

a reaction takes place. In acute cases, death may occur within the first two or three minutes, though if the patient survives long enough to reach the hospital, recovery is almost certain. Secondly, since nonmedical use of cocaine is illegal, and a person suffering from an overdose may be extremely paranoid because of the drug's action, it is unusual to find such cocaine abusers in the acute state in a hospital emergency room.

It is difficult to be certain what amount of cocaine will constitute an overdose. Amounts vary according to the authorities consulted and according to the individual concerned, since there is much individual variability. Nor can much about cocaine be said with certainty, except that it is expensive. Dr. Robert L. DuPont, director of the National Institute on Drug Abuse, notes in the foreword of the Research Monograph series booklet, *Cocaine 1977*, that "we know that cocaine can kill—not commonly but occasionally and perhaps not predictably. Despite the street lore to the contrary, death sometimes occurs even when the drug is snorted rather than injected." Dr. DuPont comments that one of the most notable aspects of our knowledge about cocaine is that so much is *not* yet known.

According to the pamphlet *All About Cocaine*, published by the Do It Now Foundation, "The two most rational statements made today regarding cocaine are (1) that most of the harsh laws covering this drug are based on the old false notion that it is highly physically addicting, and (2) that the prices charged are much too high in relation to the actual effects of the drug."*

How does cocaine affect the human body when doses are low or moderate? Cocaine is a central-nervous-system stimulant that can make introverts feel like charming and witty extroverts for a few minutes. The user experiences a "flash" or euphoric feeling that quickly passes because the cocaine is rapidly destroyed by the body. Cocaine transiently raises confidence, accelerates heartbeat, relieves fatigue, and may cause the user to become overexcited. Or it may cause very little change in feeling. Reports of subjective feelings vary with dose and with individuals. In some cases, meaningless actions are repeated again and again. Some users report happy feelings, strong psychological exultations, increases in energy, and/or other reactions. Many people who try cocaine are not sufficiently impressed to invest again the large amounts of money it costs them.

Why is cocaine so expensive? Hospitals purchase cocaine for about $35 an ounce, but street prices may range from $1,500 to $2,500 per ounce. Although the smuggler's cocaine arrives nearly 100 percent pure in the United States, wholesalers and pushers cut it with various substances such as milk sugar (lactose), powered milk, cornstarch, and local anesthetic drugs such

---

*For further information consult Do It Now Foundation, P.O. Box 5115, Phoenix, Arizona 85010, publishers of *All About Cocaine*.

as lidocaine and benzocaine. The last two drugs can cause serious irregularities of heart contractions if they are injected into the bloodstream with the cocaine, but they are not especially dangerous if sniffed or snorted. Other common adulterants, such as caffeine, are relatively harmless, but phencyclidine (PCP), a veterinary anesthetic known as angel dust, is a drug that can cause very serious problems.

Adulterants, which cut the cost to the supplier, may be much more dangerous than the cocaine itself. Buyers have no sure way of knowing what the cocaine has been cut with, and sometimes test for cocaine in a sample by putting a small amount of it on their gums. If the gums become numb, they know that they are getting either cocaine, a mixture of it with cheaper local anesthetics, or just local anesthetics with additives.

In the old days, police reportedly tweaked the noses of suspected cocaine users to find out if their noses were sensitive from sniffing this drug. Even today, cocaine is usually taken by inhaling the powder through the nasal passages ("snorting"), which irritates nasal mucous membranes. Long-term use can result in deterioration of the lining of the nose, and ultimately of the bone. The cost of cocaine on today's market is so high that it has facetiously been suggested that anyone who can afford enough cocaine to seriously damage the nose can afford a nose transplant.

Habitual users of cocaine may renew their

supplies as often as every ten minutes when they can afford to do so, for the euphoria is short lived. Some heavy users suffer deep depression when the drug's effects begin to wane and they resort to further sniffing to relieve their depression, thus creating a rapid cycle of ups and downs.

Dr. David Smith, medical director of the Haight-Ashbury Free Medical Clinic in San Francisco, California, reports the case of a person who believed cocaine to have no higher abuse potential than marijuana, and who started injecting cocaine. At the time of the report, this man was injecting, losing control, and injecting repeatedly through a four-day-and-night period. He developed a cocaine psychosis with auditory and visual hallucinations and paranoia. But not many cocaine users show up at drug treatment programs, for reasons mentioned earlier. Dr. Smith believes that this fact has misled many doctors about the abuse potential of cocaine.

Cocaine is generally regarded as not highly physically addicting, although there is tolerance in certain individuals. Withdrawal varies, too, and is usually not especially dramatic. Some authorities believe that the cause of deep depression experienced by some heavy users is a reaction to the overstimulation caused by the cocaine rather than a true withdrawal symptom. While cocaine's long-term effects on endurance seem unclear, it is certain that the drug does not save energy. It just redistributes energy, enabling one to drive the body for a long time before physical exhaustion. The comedown or "crash" may or may not be considered a form of withdrawal.

Psychological dependence is another aspect of cocaine about which there is disagreement. Most authorities report that there is good evidence that the desire to continue use when cocaine is available is remarkably strong. Some claim the abuse potential is moderately high, and others say cocaine is among the most powerfully reinforcing of all abused drugs. The U.S. government spent $4 million over a period of four years of research on cocaine, and the findings were published in *Cocaine 1977*, the report mentioned earlier. In this twenty-three page study, two of its authors, Drs. Robert Byck and Craig Van Dyke of the Yale University School of Medicine, Department of Pharmacology, conclude: "The reader may have an uneasy feeling that most of the actions and effects of cocaine that seemed to be 'known' are still open to question. This is, in fact, the case. By the nature of the acceptable evidence, we must concede that some 'facts' about cocaine's effects in man will probably never be demonstrated."

One of the few certainties about cocaine is that it is not a narcotic, though classified as such by law under the Harrison Narcotic Act of 1914. This law made cocaine users subject to the same penalties as opiate users. Today's authorities are taking a new look at this controversial and complex problem.

Amphetamines are chemicals that, like cocaine,

act as stimulants on the human body. These central-nervous-system stimulants were once popular with doctors who prescribed them for overweight patients, since they had the ability to temporarily depress appetite and allay fatigue, but their use was reexamined toward the end of the 1960s. Amphetamine abusers were common among people who received their drugs through prescription as well as those who purchased their drugs on the street. Amphetamine abusers experienced a type of psychosis like paranoid schizophrenia, which played a part in making these stimulants less popular. The hippies of the 1960s advertised "Speed Kills" to their friends, and most, but not all, doctors limited prescriptions to their patients.

One of the unusual qualities of amphetamines is their capacity to produce tolerance, a characteristic that is uncommon with central-nervous-system stimulants. Some controversy exists about the addictive qualities of amphetamines, but most people agree that psychological dependence develops in a large percentage of cases. Suicidal tendencies and actual suicides have been attributed to amphetamine abuse. Less dramatic effects include premature appearance of aging through heavy use of amphetamines that overwork the body.

Physical addiction is not well established, but there are withdrawal symptoms. These are decreased activity, sleep disturbances, and apathy that can last for months. After abrupt withdrawal of large doses, there is an increase in the percentage of rapid-eye-movement (REM) sleep, which disappears when amphetamine is given. It increases again when amphetamine is withheld. This pattern indicates the presence of some physical addiction.

In spite of the temporary help that amphetamines provide some people who need to lose weight, and for their benefit in some rare medical conditions, the abuse rate was so great that amphetamines and related compounds have come under close scrutiny in recent years. Careful control of these drugs has helped to reduce the amount available for the illegal market, and it has probably reduced the number of people who suffer from amphetamine addiction.

Jane's doctor prescribed Valium (diazepam) a popular tranquilizer, to help her adjust to her first days at college. Although most experts agree that a certain amount of tension is good, Jane persuaded her doctor that she would be better with help from a few pills. The central-nervous-system depressant that he prescribed for her appears to be relatively harmless, so the doctor did not give much thought to the matter. Jane began her pill taking the first day of registration. Since she was going to a party that evening where she did not know anyone, Jane took an extra pill. Then she drank two martinis. Although many people know that tranquilizers and alcohol do not mix because the sum of these two central-nervous-system depressants can be far greater than one plus one, Jane was not aware of this. She fell asleep at the party, and when someone woke her late in the evening, she was very embarrassed at her behavior. Combinations of tranquilizers and alcohol can produce far more tragic results, such as coma, or zombielike behavior.

Barbiturates are also central-nervous-system depressants and they must never be combined with alcoholic beverages because of the extreme danger that such a combination may cause death. Alcohol, tranquilizers, and barbiturates all slow down such functions as breathing, heartbeat, reasoning, sensory powers, and thinking. When tranquilizers or barbiturates are taken in combination with alcohol, the reaction in the body is greater than the sum of the two drugs if taken separately. Most tranquilizer-related deaths have been caused by combinations of these drugs with alcohol. Barbiturates are often used by suicidal persons in doses that cause death without the help of alcohol, but smaller doses combined with alcohol can be the cause of accidental death.

Alcohol, barbiturates, and tranquilizers, alone or in combination, are neither good nor bad, moral nor immoral. The user or the abuser determines such qualities. Lack of knowledge about drugs and combinations of drugs causes more damage to the human body than many people realize, especially when addiction is involved.

For most people, alcohol is not addictive and may never be a problem. In moderate amounts, the indirect effect of alcohol on the body is usually one of stimulation that produces a mood of emotional freedom. Most people who drink do so in a responsible manner by carefully choosing the time, place, and amount. With alcohol, as with many other drugs, one usually gets from it what is expected. In other words, if people drink socially to enjoy a situation, they usually control the drinking so that the situation continues to be enjoyable. If people set out to get drunk, they usually do just that, even though the amount they drink may be the same as that of the social drinkers.

Have you ever met an alcoholic who claims that s/he has hardly ever taken a drug? Since alcohol is widely accepted and can be bought without prescription, alcohol has been held in a separate class from other drugs to which people become addicted. The alcohol addict is seldom referred to as such, but the hallmarks of true addiction are present in such people. Tolerance with withdrawal are characteristic and even well recognized. Most people who drink alcohol do not become alcoholics, but for those who become addicted, alcohol is a very dangerous depressive drug. The incidence of alcohol addiction in the United States is estimated at 9 or 10 million people, but the true figure may never be known.

The progress from social drinking to addictive drinking is usually gradual, following a different pace for different people. It varies over a period from one to twenty-five years, with an average of ten to twenty-five years.

While the progression to becoming an alcoholic is somewhat different for each individual, many alcoholics can identify with a common pattern. Take John for example. John has been a social drinker since high school. In college, he began drinking to ease the stress of impending exams, social problems, and other kinds of tension. The alcohol helped to relieve the stress and provided a euphoric state after which he slept. His "morning after" hangovers from his drinking bouts were unpleasant, but not unpleasant enough to stop him from increasing the amount of alcohol needed to produce the effect he felt was helpful in difficult situations. This successful activity was repeated again and again, while increasing tolerance made it necessary to increase the amounts. John noticed that he had memory blackouts, a condition in which he completely forgot what had happened during his drinking episodes on previous nights. His friends remarked about his excessive drinking, so, from time to time, John would sneak a drink. He acted as bartender for friends, so he could have a few drinks from the bottle without being noticed. John frequently drove while drunk and on one occasion he nearly had a serious accident. Since John had set a rule that he would not drink before noon he found himself anxiously waiting for that time to come. Only alcoholics drink in the morning, he told himself.

At this stage, John began to feel guilty about the way he drank, realizing that he was behaving differently from his friends. He found vague excuses for having a drink, and managed to gulp his drinks since he was not sure when the opportunity for another supply of alcohol would arise. By this time, John realized that he could not control his drinking, and his guilt feelings made him resentful and aggressive. He made many resolutions to stop, but they all failed, and this failure added to his unreasonable and irritable behavior. John began to isolate himself from friends and family, and these people, in turn, turned away from John, who was now an unpleasant person. Such behavior made John even more depressed, and he turned even more often to alcoholic beverages, which appeared to him to be the only friend he had left. He dropped out of college, since he could no longer keep up with the work. His mornings were filled with nursing hangovers and his afternoons and evenings were spent in drinking.

Time and time again, John promised himself he would stop drinking but he succeeded for only brief periods of time. By now, his eating habits were poor and his general health suffered. John began drinking in bars with other people who spent much time there. These people had little in common with John other than their liking for alcohol.

Sometimes, John was paranoid. There were vague fears, tremors, and other health problems along with the morning hangovers. Sometimes the mornings began with a drink. Financial problems, health problems, social problems all combined to make John admit that he had hit "rock bottom." At this point he asked for help for the alcoholism he knew he could not handle.

Not every alcohol addict goes through all the steps that John did. Some reach for help before they isolate themselves from family and friends. Others do so before there is serious physical deterioration. But the pattern of becoming an alcoholic is a familiar one. Acknowledgment of dependence on alcohol is difficult, but recovery may come sooner when people in the environment of the person who is drinking too much understand the need for help and avoid stigmatizing the alcoholic. While the road to alcoholism remains much the same today as in the past, the age at which young people are beginning to drink heavily has changed, and the pace at which they are becoming alcoholics is faster.

Take the case of Betty, who began drinking beer from her family's refrigerator at the age of nine. She and her sister wanted to see what it was like to get drunk. When they first experimented they got sick. After a while, they managed to build up a tolerance, and they drank often. Betty's older sister was upset with what was happening to her and she joined Alcoholics Anonymous, where she found help. But Betty continued to drink so she could feel a part of the good times at parties. Over the years she continued to drink excessively even while pregnant, creating a dangerous situation for her unborn child. Betty may have to experience more hard times before she is ready to ask for help.

Chris does not realize he is an alcoholic because he believes that he cannot be one unless he drinks more than beer and fruity wines. His idea of an alcoholic is an old bum in a doorway clutching a bottle.

Many people believe that there are few alcoholics in countries where wine is customarily taken with meals, as in France and Italy. Drinking is socially acceptable in both countries, but France is higher than Italy on lists showing the percentage of people who are alcoholics. This may be due to the fact that many French sip wine at interludes during the day for relaxation while Italians tend to confine it to meals and socializing. In countries where wine replaces water and milk as a table beverage, many children are introduced to it at an early age. Those who think that wine and beer cannot be responsible for alcoholism do not realize that the quantity of alcohol, not the kind of beverage, is a very important factor. For example, a six-pack of beer contains enough alcohol to cause a driver to be legally classified as a drunken driver.

How much is not the only important factor in the development of alcohol addiction. *Why* a person drinks is another measure of whether or not s/he has or is developing a drinking problem. Here are twenty questions that are often used to help in the recognition of alcoholism or its approach:

1. Do you start the day with a drink?
2. Do you go to school or work when intoxicated?
3. Does drinking interfere with your home life?
4. Do you feel guilty after drinking?
5. Do you drink because you are shy?
6. Do you drink to forget problems?
7. Do friends, employers, and/or close family criticize your drinking?
8. Do you make excuses for having another drink?
9. Do you crave a drink at the same time each day?

10. Has drinking affected your reputation?
11. Do you want a drink the morning after a drinking bout?
12. Does drinking interfere with your sleep?
13. Have you come into conflict with the law because of drinking?
14. Have you driven a car while drunk?
15. Do you undergo dramatic personality changes after drinking?
16. Do you require medical attention or suffer frequent physical discomfort because of drinking?
17. Do you drink to escape loneliness?
18. Do you drink alone?
19. Are you less efficient or less ambitious because of increased drinking patterns?
20. Have you suffered memory blackouts?

If you answer yes to three of these questions, you should seek help. Even one is a warning.

There is no doubt that alcohol is the drug that causes alcoholism, but there is much disagreement about why some people can drink large amounts of it without becoming alcoholics. At one time it was popular to talk about an *alcoholic personality* with characteristics such as dependency and immaturity. Alcoholics have been described as angry people who do not know they are angry and do not show this feeling except when they have released the feeling through drunkenness. Their anger is believed to have been born of frustration due to a lack of a maturing of their dependent feelings. According to this theory, such adults continue to rely on others in a childlike manner. They need immediate satisfaction and they demand instant gratification the way young children do. Adult alcoholics may be searching for unconditional love, something that can never be obtained. Repeated rebuffs in this search make anger and frustration inescapable. But even those experts who consider alcoholics to have many common personality characteristics admit that the roots of alcoholism remain a mystery.

The causes of alcohol addiction are very complex, with influences from social, physiological, and cultural factors. Dr. Donald W. Goodwin and his colleagues at Washington University in St. Louis have been studying the relationship between heredity and alcoholism for many years. In one study, it was found that sons of alcoholics were four times more likely to become alcoholic than the sons of nondrinkers. This was true whether or not they were raised by their parents. By studying children of alcoholics who were adopted, it was possible to rule out some of the environmental influences. New evidence seems to indicate that hereditary factors either do not exist in women as they may in men, or that they are masked by cultural factors that tend to repress susceptibility.

The relationship between alcohol and heredity is still a subject of controversy, and experts who accept genes as a factor do not consider heredity the whole cause. Studies have shown that one-fourth to one-half of all alcoholic persons have had an alcoholic parent or close relative, according to the National Clearinghouse for Alcoholism Information. In a recent survey done for the National Institute on Alcohol Abuse and Alcoholism, the conclusions indicated that the children of alcoholic parents are twice as likely to become alcoholics as the children of nonalcoholic parents. The influence of environment may well play a part here, but since there are an estimated 28 million children of alcoholic persons in the United States today, the importance of prevention of this type of addiction is quite obvious.

While little is known about the physiological basis of alcoholism, some researchers feel that people who become alcoholics have different metabolisms from other people. According to one theory, an "error in metabolism" makes these individuals need more vitamins, and when they taste alcohol, their vitamin deficiency initiates a craving. There are specialists who believe an endocrine gland problem is involved in alcoholism. Recent experiments with rats indicate that a chemical known as tetrahydropapaveroline may be involved in alcoholism, and brain chemistry is a factor. Certainly, the roots of this kind of addiction are complex.

Probably about one person in fifteen who begins drinking eventually becomes an alcoholic. With a small percentage of people, the social-drinking phase does not exist, for they become chronic alcoholics as soon as they begin to drink. Whether this is due to some kind of chemical imbalance, to the presence or absence of a certain chemical in the body, or to an individual reaction to relief from stress that is so well liked that it causes the experience to be repeated again and again, no one knows. But it is known that instant alcoholics do exist.

Today, young problem drinkers are not uncommon. In fact, the estimated number of problem drinkers between the ages of twelve and seventeen is 1.3 million. Of these, a half million or more may be alcoholics. Children as young as eight and nine years of age register at clinics for alcohol detoxification. A report from New York City schools estimates that about 10 percent of the students in junior and senior high schools are either potential alcoholics or alcoholics.

It is hard to grasp such figures, but if there is just one person with an alcohol problem who is closely related to you, you know that there is great cause for concern. The U.S. government calls alcoholism the number-one health problem in the nation.

Addiction to alcohol is a problem for the alcoholic, and it is also a problem for families, communities, the state, and the nation. The estimated 9 million alcoholics closely touch the lives of about 40 million other people. The National Congress of Parents and Teachers believes that problem drinking far surpasses all other forms of drug abuse and addiction as a menace to public health. In cooperation with the United States Department of Health, Education and

Welfare they have published *Alcohol: A Family Affair*,* in which there are suggestions for the prevention of alcoholism by the development of responsible drinking patterns.

Alcoholics Anonymous is well known for its help to alcoholics' families as well as to the alcoholics themselves. Al-Anon (for adult family members) and Alateen (for teenage children of alcoholics) deal with problems that arise in a family where a parent has a drinking problem.

The treatment approaches available for alcoholics of all ages vary greatly. In addition to Alcoholics Anonymous, there are treatments based on individual counseling, group therapy, psychodrama, drug therapy, medication (such as antabuse, which causes illness when any alcohol is consumed). And there are programs that look into the alcoholic's past and some that are concerned only with the future. There are treatment centers that use hypnotic suggestion and some that experiment with electric shock and/or drugs to make alcoholic beverages unattractive. In the United States alone, the number of treatment centers for alcoholics is estimated at 7,500. Many use a combination of techniques. Finding the kind of program to fit an individual alcoholic can be bewildering. Studies show that some of the most effective treatment methods are those in which the individuals carry

---

Alcohol: A Family Affair, DHEW Publication No. (ADM) 74-75, U.S. Government Printing Office, Washington, D.C., 1974.

much of the responsibility for actively helping themselves.

So little is known about the cause or cure of alcoholism that much emphasis is being placed on education and prevention. Many myths still surround alcoholism, although progress is being made in the attitude of communities about alcoholism. Many people who readily accept nicotine and caffeine addicts still hold prejudices against alcoholics. The moral connection with drinking of alcoholic beverages makes it difficult for some individuals to admit that they cannot tolerate alcohol. They would freely admit that they cannot drink coffee at night, or that chocolate candy does not agree with them. While cancer, mental retardation, tuberculosis, and other conditions that once were stigmatized have become more understandable, and early treatment has been made available, the early stages of alcoholism are sometimes subject to the misconduct concept. As progress continues toward understanding of alcoholism, those who suffer from this disorder tend to seek help in the earlier stages.

Barbiturate addicts seldom suffer from condemnation when they begin their drug taking by medical prescriptions. Barbiturates are yesterday's tranquilizers. About a dozen kinds are used medically in the United States. The differences among them concern such matters as the speed and duration of the effect, and they are roughly divided into three groups: (1) the short-acting barbiturates (secobarbital, pentobarbital);

(2) the intermediate-acting barbiturates (butabarbital, amobarbital); and (3) the long-acting barbiturates (phenobarbital). All are depressants. Phenobarbital can accumulate in the body when used repeatedly. All have the potential for addiction, but the great majority of people who are given barbiturates by doctors never develop dependence on them. Long-acting barbiturates, generally used for daytime sedation, are far less addicting than short-term ones, which are used for inducing sleep or are abused for mood changing by those who obtain them without prescription. There is some disagreement about whether tolerance can develop when barbiturates are taken in low doses repeatedly. When large doses are taken daily for six weeks or more, they produce severe physical dependence that is very dangerous. Abrupt withdrawal often results in stupor, convulsions, coma, and even death.

Psychological dependence is known to develop even with small doses prescribed by doctors. Middle-aged women appear to be the most common victims of this kind of addiction, and one finds these addicts going from doctor to doctor asking for their drug of choice. When they stop taking their pills, the mild symptoms of withdrawal from therapeutic doses, similar to alcoholic withdrawal, are sometimes confused with the symptoms that made the women begin taking the drugs.

Young people who abuse barbiturates, as well as some adults who take them by prescription, frequently use them in combination with stimulants. Since the barbiturates produce depression, this is not surprising. It is believed that many suicides by barbiturates are accidental. When people who take these drugs regularly increase their doses, they become confused and may not remember how much they have taken. Then they take more to relieve their depression or to try to bring about a desired mood, and accidentally overdose.

Barbiturate addicts appear to be mentally confused, slow, forgetful, and have poor ability to concentrate or remember. Slurred speech and giddiness may also be present. Barbiturate dependence has been compared with alcoholism, and the state of intoxication is often referred to as a barbiturate drunk. Breaking the addiction to barbiturates is so difficult that many therapeutic communities that accept heroin users reject barbiturate addicts because they relapse so frequently. Unfortunately, there is no known drug to replace the craving as methadone does in the case of heroin addiction.

Methaqualone is a central-nervous-system depressant that was originally thought to have many of the good properties of the barbiturates without the potential for addiction. It was found to have very desirable mood-changing qualities, and it became much abused as an illicit drug. It is commonly known under such names as Sopors, Quaaludes, Somnifac, Parest, and Mandrax, but since it is both psychologically and physiologically addicting, many physicians have changed their opinion of it as a possible substitute for barbiturates.

In 1977, the U.S. Office of Drug Abuse Policy considered the problem of illicit barbiturate use a major area of concern and looked into the possibility of removing barbiturates from the market and replacing them with alternative, safer medications. The federal government's most recent survey of the behavior of barbiturate users revealed that each year approximately 3 million Americans use them without proper medical supervision. Further, several hundreds of thousands of these users take them to the point where they are suffering serious psychological and physical effects.

Barbiturate use in medicine became less popular with the advent of tranquilizers, which now are very widely used. Even about ten years ago, when the production in the United States reached 800,000 pounds for barbiturates, 1.5 million pounds of tranquilizers were produced. Whether or not tranquilizers have addicting properties is the subject of much controversy. It is well established that some have a specific capacity to diminish or reverse disordered thought processes in schizophrenic or psychotic patients. Certain tranquilizers appear to have calming effects and to promote sleep when hospital patients are agitated or suffer from insomnia. But most of the people who take tranquilizers are the so-called "walking wounded." According to a study by the National Commission on

Marijuana and Drug Abuse, one person in six takes some form of tranquilizer regularly. Millions of prescriptions are written annually for Valium, the most popular prescribed drug in the United States. Tranquilizers such as Valium are high on lists of the most abused drugs, along with nicotine and alcohol. Whether they are obtained with or without prescriptions, tranquilizers are found in the medicine chests of large numbers of people.

Many doctors believe that tranquilizers are not addictive, and they have been prescribing them to such a degree that there is mass sedation. Parents have been known to give young children some of their own tranquilizers to calm them when they feel anxious or jittery. People of all ages think of tranquilizers as "all-problem solving" pills.

Tighter regulations on Valium and some other drugs were put into effect by the Food and Drug Administration; these limit refills to five over a period of six months. A physician must prescribe again after the fifth refill if more of the drug is needed.

Perhaps the confusion about the potential for addiction with tranquilizers is partly due to the fact that different people react in different ways to chemicals. It is also due to the fact that some tranquilizers may be addictive while others may not be. Only a few are mentioned here.

Opinions range widely on the addiction potential of Valium. Many doctors believe that it is virtually nonaddictive. Others note that physical dependence occurs with high doses over long periods of time. At least one highly respected psychiatrist considers Valium as the most addictive drug in common, legal use. Certainly, there is little doubt that it is commonly used, and there is some agreement that there might be a degree of tolerance, but relatively few authorities consider the potential for addiction high or the drug lethal even in large doses, unless it is combined with another drug.

Librium (chlordiazepoxide) is chemically related to Valium, and it, too, is used in the treatment of anxiety and tension states. With Librium, as with Valium, tolerance varies. Just as some people get drunk on one alcoholic beverage, there are people who are especially sensitive to Valium and Librium. A common evaluation of the addiction potential of Valium and Librium is: "possible with heavy, prolonged use."

Meprobamate, which is commonly known as Miltown and Equanil, was widely used when it was first marketed well over a decade ago. This tranquilizer produces a pronounced relaxing effect on muscles. With small doses, it relieves anxiety without producing drowsiness, and this is a desirable quality that is rather rare. However, when large doses are taken, serious withdrawal can result with symptoms that include convulsions and even death. When used in excessive doses, there have been reports of drowsiness, motor incoordination, staggering, slurred speech, and mental confusion. In a number of cases there have been rage reactions. These unpleasant symptoms occurred only when meprobamate was used at doses higher than those prescribed by physicians. The addiction potential is considered heavy when used as a street drug, and its high overdose potential concerns physicians. In addition to these problems, it has been found to have less value in treatment of anxiety than some of the other tranquilizers.

So although alcohol, barbiturates, and tranquilizers all depress the central nervous system, one can see that they vary greatly from drug to drug in their potential for addiction. Even the opinions about their addictive properties vary. Many different kinds of drugs are being used in combinations, and this affects the properties of each. According to a recent report on world drug abuse prepared by the United Nations Division of Narcotics Abuse, the most commonly involved drugs of those used in combination are alcohol, barbiturates, and marijuana.

Marijuana is a preparation of the dried leaves, seeds, and flowering tops of the Indian hemp plant, *Cannabis sativa*, which is one of the oldest and most widely used mind-altering drugs known. Hashish, which is the brown resin extracted from the tops of high quality cannabis plants, is often five or six times stronger than marijuana. However, strong marijuana may be more potent than poor quality hashish.

The health consequences and possible addictive potential of marijuana are a large part of the marijuana controversy, a complex social issue. Dr. Robert L. DuPont, director of the National Institute on Drug Abuse, comments in the 1976 report, *Marihuana and Health*, that the realization that many users of legal substances suffer ill effects while many users of prohibited substances have no problems with their use has strained our national capacity to deal rationally with some of the issues involved.[*]

[*]*Marihuana and Health*, Sixth Annual Report to the U.S. Congress from the Secretary of Health, Education, and Welfare, 1976, page iv.

Is marijuana addictive? A Gallup poll reported in 1977 that 59 percent of the public believed that this drug was physically addictive. If one polled the experts then or now, few would agree with the public. While there is still much to learn about marijuana, the problem of physical addiction does not loom large. Users do not become "hooked on marijuana" the way many people think. While some tolerance develops with long-term, heavy use, withdrawal symptoms are absent in the concentration commonly used in the United States.

Even though most of the public may be under the wrong impression about addiction for those who use it for recreational purposes, there is some potential for psychological addiction, especially among people who have had emotional problems prior to use.

According to the *Non-Medical Use of Drugs: Interim Report of the Canadian Government Commission of Inquiry,* a similar type of dependence occurs regularly in our society "with respect to such things as television, music, books, religion, sex, money, favorite foods, certain drugs, hobbies, sports or games, and, often, other persons."* Long-term heavy marijuana use has been reported to produce a type of psychological dependence, with symptoms such as insomnia, restlessness, and irritability when use is stopped. These symptoms do not require medical attention,

---

*The Non-Medical Use of Drugs: The Interim Report of the Canadian Government Commission of Inquiry Penguin Books 1971, p. 46.

according to the nonprofit organization, the Drug Abuse Council, of Washington, D.C. 20036.

Some emotionalism about marijuana is dying due to the number of people who have tried the drug without apparent harm. This number may be more than 36 million. Fifteen million people use it on a moderate basis and about three million use it daily. The old idea of marijuana as a "killer weed," causing murder, rape, and insanity, probably has relatively few supporters. Even people with minimal knowledge about the drug are becoming aware that marijuana tends to calm people rather than make them excited or violent. But possession of small amounts of marijuana is still a crime in many states, and the legal question is one of the reasons that the government has been conducting extensive research on health and marijuana.

While the picture regarding marijuana use is far from complete, there is good evidence that moderate use is far less harmful than once thought, though it has not been given a completely clean bill of health. With a continual escalation in the amount of marijuana use likely, it seems highly probable that more individuals with impaired psychological and/or physical conditions will be involved. The implications for them may be quite different than for occasional users who are in optimal health. This is one of the factors being considered by the government of the United States in the quest for a rational social policy.

The truth about marijuana and health is mired in

numerous conflicting reports. Much of the research in the past has been scientifically flawed, with results that are impossible to duplicate. While research continues to explore the effects of chronic and heavy use over a long term, a number of states have decriminalized the possession of small amounts of marijuana. This means that in these states a person may be fined but is not subject to a criminal record or jail sentence. The National Organization for the Reform of Marijuana Laws (NORML) has done much to bring about such action. It supports decriminalization but does not encourage the use of marijuana. In fact, this organization fully supports a discouragement policy toward the recreational use of all drugs, including alcohol, tobacco, and marijuana. Its members believe that criminal penalties should not be applied against those who use such drugs, and they are supported by a great many organizations.

The American Bar Association, American Public Health Association, National Council of Churches, B'nai B'rith, Governing Board of the American Medical Association, National Education Association, American Academy of Pediatrics, National Association for Mental Health, Official State Study Commissions of California, Illinois, Maine, Massachusetts, Michigan, New Jersey, Pennsylvania, Virginia, and Wisconsin, and many other organizations and individuals support NORML. For more information, contact NORML, 2317 M Street, N.W., Washington, D.C. 20037.

In the debate over whether penalties for possession of marijuana are too harsh, the following basic question has been suggested: Whatever you might feel about marijuana, the legal issue is—do you think the police and courts should spend time and money prosecuting users and sending them to prison? The FBI Uniform Crime Report for 1975 indicates that seven out of every ten drug arrests were for marijuana. Annual cost estimates for arrests and prosecution are estimated at $600 million. And there is always the problem of the mechanism for discouragement being more damaging to the individual than the drug itself.

Those who sit in prison for marijuana offenses feel bitter about the fact that they are criminals, while people who ignore the warnings of lung cancer from cigarettes and those who drink to excess are free to do as they wish with their drugs of choice. But even if moderate use of marijuana is less harmful than tobacco addiction and alcoholism, many people feel that legalizing another drug has little to do with harmful effects of those that are already legal. Decriminalization, however, does not appear to increase the use of marijuana, and represents a compromise measure to stop senseless and tragic arrest while a rational, well thought out, long term marijuana policy is developed.

What are the physical effects of marijuana? Actually, they vary a great deal, depending on the individual user, the set (expectations), the physical environment, the concentration of the active chemical (tetrahydrocannabinol, or THC), and other factors. Different environmental factors during the growing process of marijuana plants and different methods of preparing marijuana affect the concentration of the active chemical. Accurate experiments can only be carried out with known amounts of THC. Even when the pure form of this chemical is isolated and used in preparations of known concentration, one must consider the comparatively minor effects from related compounds in the plants.

Few plants appear to be so variable or unpredictable as marijuana and its extracts. Two different reference samples have been prepared for scientific studies by the UN laboratory: the marijuana type that contains 2.6 percent THC and a more potent type, resembling hashish, with 7.4 percent THC. Adding to the confusion in experimental studies, there are marked differences in the amount of active chemical in the average daily dose of smokers in different countries. For example, the average THC consumption among daily users of marijuana in the United States has been estimated at 5 to 10 milligrams. In India and North Africa, where hashish is more popular, the average daily dosage probably ranges from 13 to 66 milligrams. No wonder the reports of the effects of THC vary greatly from country to country.

Here is another aspect that makes experimental studies difficult. The majority of smokers of nicotine cigarettes and marijuana find that the ritual of smoking reduces anxiety and reinforces the effect of the drug. Dr. Gary Greenberg of the psychology department of Wichita State University in Kansas reports on ritual's role in *Addictions*,* a publication of the Addiction Research Foundation of Ontario, Canada. Dr. Greenberg feels there is substantial evidence that the experience of being high with marijuana is more dependent on subjective factors than previously believed. The high depends on a complex interaction of the social setting (the friends or absence of them, and the place), the physical stimuli within the setting (soft lights, music, incense), the set or expectations of the user, and the user's personality, as well as the concentration of THC and related chemicals.

Many people who try marijuana for the first time do not experience the euphoria, and this seems to support the theory that a marijuana user learns to get high through frequent participation in the rituals. There have been occasions when frequent marijuana smokers felt themselves to be high even when they smoked a placebo in experiments. Since they did not know there was any THC present, they reacted as they would have if it had been present because they were conditioned to react that way. This does not mean that marijuana does not have a physical effect on the human body, but it does indicate that scientific experimentation on the effects of marijuana in different individuals is difficult indeed.

The following physical effects appear to be com-

---

*Gary Greenberg, "The Real High: Ritual's Role in the Marijuana Experience," *Addictions*, vol. 23, no. 4 (Winter 1976), p. 55.

mon for the so-called average user. Physiological and psychoactive effects appear in 2 to 3 minutes after smoking and last for about 90 to 120 minutes, with the peak effect occurring about 10 to 20 minutes after smoking. While subjective effects vary greatly with factors mentioned earlier, people who smoke occasionally with friends in a setting that is free from anxiety report a state of dreamy well-being and a change in their perception of the flow of time. Muscle weakness is a common reaction, as is a decrease in feelings of aggressiveness. High doses can produce stupor, and panic reactions.

Among American users, the most common adverse psychological reaction is an acute panic anxiety reaction. In this situation, an individual becomes acutely anxious and loses perspective. This reaction appears to be more common in relatively inexperienced users, although it has been experienced by regular users when an unexpectedly high dose is involved. Such symptoms usually respond to firm assurance from a friend or authority figure and wear off as the effect of the drug diminishes.

Research about marijuana and health continues on many fronts. There are still unresolved questions about the possible adverse impact of marijuana on the body's immune responses, basic cell metabolism, hormone levels, and other biological functions. Evidence is fragmentary and incomplete in all these areas.

In *Marihuana and Health*, concern is expressed

that heavy chronic marijuana use could well lead to lung impairment similar to that found in heavy cigarette smokers, with the same heightened susceptibility to heart disease, lung cancer, and emphysema.*

In the same report, emphasis is placed on the hazards of driving while under the influence of marijuana. Dr. DuPont states in the foreword, "We know that marihuana intoxication poses a significant threat to highway safety in much the same way as alcohol does. The exact size of that threat remains a matter for conjecture. Many marihuana users report driving while intoxicated and since we know driving skills are impaired under those circumstances, the problem is real."

Later in the report it is noted that "a continuing danger common to both driving and flying is that some of the perceptual or other performance decrements resulting from marihuana use may persist for some time (possibly several hours) beyond the period of subjective intoxication. Under such circumstances, the individual may attempt to fly or drive without realization that his or her ability to do so is still impaired although he or she no longer feels high."**

Tests on driving skills after marijuana use show definite impairment. A significant dose-related increase in braking time has been found. The time re-

*Marihuana and Health, Sixth Annual Report to the U.S. Congress from the Secretary of Health, Education, and Welfare, 1976, p. 15.
**Marihuana and Health, p. 24.

quired for recovery from glare when driving at night increases, and this effect lasts for several hours after smoking marijuana. These factors, together with lack of inhibition and false judgment as to actual ability, and failure to recognize and thus correct errors, combine to result in seriously impaired performance at a time when the individual feels super-competent.

One of the concerns about marijuana use among the young is expressed in the same government report as follows: "Marihuana is most widely used by adolescents and young adults during critical stages in their personality development and while developing intellectual and psychosocial skills. To what extent, if any, chronic intoxication affects development is still unknown. While the percentage of the population which uses marihuana heavily on a daily basis is still a small minority even in this group, any serious consequences of use may well be expected to have implications for extended periods of their lives."*

Addiction is apparently one of the less important issues in the marijuana controversy, but since so many people have been exposed to the wrong information about this subject, no book on addictions would be complete without a discussion of the subject.

*Marihuana and Health, p. 2

While the theories about the causes of heroin addiction and the best methods of prevention and treatment are being debated, the number of people addicted to heroin grows. During a three-year period from 1973 to 1976, the estimated number of heroin addicts in the United States doubled, bringing the figure to 800,000. Large cities account for over 500,000 narcotic addicts, according to a recent survey conducted in conjunction with the Drug Abuse Council, and the National League of Cities/United States Conference of Mayors. About half the heroin addicts are thought to live in the New York City area, where their average consumption is believed to be $100 worth of drugs per day. If the present increase in the use of narcotics is left unchecked, there are predictions that heroin addiction will spread to the smallest township in the United States. But such statistics are meaningless compared with the true meaning of narcotic addiction in human terms.

Addiction to narcotics such as heroin is considered the classic form of addiction even by those people who accept the term only in its narrowest sense. As mentioned in Chapter 1, tolerance is a factor with narcotics; a user must gradually increase the amount of the drug to produce the same feeling of euphoria that was once obtained by smaller amounts. Withdrawal is suffered by those who have developed tolerance and these symptoms have been described in varied terms, ranging from extremely severe suffering to symptoms somewhat like a bad case of flu. Craving is characteristic of users, with estimates of the time and amount of drug use needed for addiction varying greatly. The craving that lasts long after the physical dependence has disappeared is particularly high with narcotics. Many former heroin addicts report a periodic craving that persists for ten or more years after any physical addiction. People who have given up their smoking addictions and crave cigarettes for a year or more afterward tend to be more sympathetic to addicts in treatment than people who have never experienced a craving of this sort.

While most people have some idea what heroin is, many are vague about how it is related to opium, morphine, and poppies. Actually, heroin is a chemical known as diacetylmorphine, produced synthetically from morphine. Morphine comes from the opium poppy, *Papaver somniferum*. This species of poppy is native to the Middle East and Southeast Asia but is grown in Mexico and other parts of the world. For about seven to ten days each year the plant produces a white milky substance, which becomes reddish brown and gummy when it dries in contact with the air. Further drying and powdering produces opium. About twenty-five organic substances are found in opium and a number of drugs are obtained from it. Morphine is the major one, but codeine, papaverine, and noscapine are other drugs found naturally in opium. Heroin is produced by exposing morphine to acetic acid. It was introduced in 1898 as a "nonaddictive" substitute for morphine, but by 1903 the fact that heroin itself was strongly addictive was widely recognized. The illegal production of heroin is a profitable, long-established criminal activity.

The chemical heroin is diluted for street sales with substances such as lactose (milk sugar), quinine, and other foreign materials so that less than 2 percent heroin may remain. Ignorance of the strength of the heroin is probably the most frequent cause of overdose in heroin addicts. Each time users purchase heroin, they must risk its being of different strength from what their bodies are accustomed to and can tolerate. A sudden and sizable increase can be fatal.

The fact that heroin addicts die at younger ages and in higher ratio to the general population is not surprising. A number of studies indicate that the chances of a heroin addict dying in any one year is between 2 and 6 percent. In addition to the possibility of overdosing, heroin addicts suffer from deaths due to medical complications from foreign substances that they take into their bodies along with the heroin, and they suffer from a higher rate of suicide than the average population. Heroin and morphine (from which heroin is prepared), produce minimal physical complications from a medical viewpoint if dosage is controlled.

When heroin reaches the brain, it is converted into morphine, a central-nervous-system depressant. So, in a sense, the heroin epidemic is a morphine epidemic. The first narcotic epidemic in the United States occurred at the time of the Civil War, when morphine was used widely as a painkiller for soldiers. In fact, morphine addiction became known as the soldier's disease. Toward the end of the nineteenth century, many patent medicines contained significant amounts of opiate drugs, and a fairly large number of people became addicted to them. Medicines such as Dr. Barton's Brown Mixture, Dover's Powder, Mrs. Winslow's Soothing Syrup, and Ayer's Cherry Pectoral made them feel better. There were teething syrups for young children and soothing syrups for a wide variety of illnesses which contained narcotics. Godfrey's Cordial was a mixture of opium, molasses, and sassafras that was extremely popular and was given to thousands of infants by parents who were unaware of the addiction potential of the opium in it.

As people became aware of the growth of a fairly large opiate-dependent population in the United States and saw that the patent medicines were being used by people who appeared addicted to them, the medical profession began to exercise restraints in prescribing narcotics. In 1906 the Pure Food and Drug Act forced the labeling of patent medicines containing opiates and other "dangerous" drugs.

In 1914 the U.S. Congress passed the Harrison Narcotic Act, which was considered an effort to control drug abuse through the use of the government's taxing power. At this point in time, the purchase or possession of narcotic drugs for nonmedical reasons became a criminal offense, and many addicts were left without medical care. The confusion between drug addiction as an illness and as an illegal act remains, but in the early 1970s, penalties for possession of drugs were placed under the control of the Department of Justice, with some provisions for rehabilitation and education. Research was increased in some areas, but much more is needed.

Basic brain research in recent years has led to valuable information about the way morphinelike drugs act on the nervous system. The stage for further discoveries in this field was set when scientists learned that opiates suppress pain by acting on specific sites on cell membranes, known as opiate receptors. Cell membranes were formerly called cell walls, but scientists have found that they do far more than keep the contents of the cell inside. Along with other functions, they control which chemicals can and cannot enter. Receptor sites on cell membranes have been compared with locks that accept only the keys that fit them, or doorways through which only familiar relatives or friends are permitted to pass. Suppose your doctor has given you morphine to relieve extreme pain after an operation. The molecules of morphine circulate in your bloodstream until they reach places in your brain where they can enter because they fit receptors much as keys fit certain locks.

By making very slight chemical changes in molecules that are related to morphine, biochemists have learned that certain synthetic chemicals can serve as the "key in the lock" of opiate receptors. However, they produce different effects from morphine. For example, when a small group of atoms is either added or subtracted, the new kind of molecule may be a synthetic drug that blocks the action of morphine. Such a drug, like naloxone, acts as an antagonist, or blocking agent. Naloxone is used in emergency rooms to relieve dangerous conditions from heroin and other opiate overdoses. Since naloxone acts very rapidly, it may be that this drug has a greater affinity for a person's opiate receptors than heroin or morphine. Naloxone is also used in treatment programs for people who are addicted to heroin.

Cyclazocine, another antagonist that blocks the effects of heroin, has been used even more extensively than naloxone in treating heroin addicts. A study of another antagonist, known as naltrexone, began in 1973 at New York Medical College under the direction of Dr. Richard B. Resnick. This antagonist became preferred over some of the others because of its potency and longer duration of action and the U.S. government began extensive testing of it for use in treatment programs. Antagonists make it impossible for heroin to give the euphoric effect the addict seeks, but they do not stop the anxiety, tension, frustration, and craving that the heroin relieves. As a result, many patients in such programs discontinue taking the antagonists and return to black-market heroin.

Methadone, another synthetic drug, blocks the effect of heroin by acting as a substitute rather than an antagonist. It is sometimes called an agonist. The fact that methadone is addicting has been considered both good and bad. Patients do not drop out of treatment readily, since they are addicted to the methadone. This gives the therapists who run some methadone-maintenance programs time to help their patients develop new life-styles with alternative satisfactions. Therapy, job training, education, new friends, are all part of a heroin addict's rehabilitation. Since methadone is taken by mouth, it breaks the needle habit that is part of the addictive ritual with heroin and which is a cause of many diseases such as hepatitis, septicemia, abscesses, and internal infections. Getting drugs from a clinic is more socially acceptable, so this, too, is part of the rehabilitation. The person now becomes a patient taking prescribed drugs daily rather than an addict who is evading the law and who usually must steal in order to secure a supply of even questionable quality and concentration that is needed every four to six hours.

In addition to these benefits, methadone not only blocks the effect of heroin, it produces no euphoria when properly administered. This permits the person who is stabilized on methadone to function as a person who is not addicted to an opiate and eliminates the temptation to revert to the heroin-seeking lifestyle.

While methadone is not the perfect answer for those who want release from heroin addiction, it appears to be one of the best, if not the best, at present. About 90,000 patients are in methadone programs. Many of these people have been rehabilitated so that they can return to school, hold jobs, and live lives that they find meaningful. But thousands of addicts who want treatment are on waiting lists. While only a fraction of drug abusers seek or are steered into treatment programs, declining budgets make it difficult for those who do want help to find places either in methadone-maintenance programs, in drug-free residential treatment centers, or in community-based programs.

For some who want help, treatment stops after methadone is used in decreasing doses until the person no longer needs drugs to prevent withdrawal. For still others methadone is given daily without therapy. Programs that include therapy and other rehabilitation services have a much better chance of succeeding than those that just administer methadone, but they are expensive. However, when one considers the cost of keeping a heroin addict in prison or the cost to society when an addict supports his/her habit by crime, the cost of methadone maintenance with

therapy and of other programs that contribute to rehabilitation is small.

Weaning an addict from drug use is a subject of
much controversy. While many staff workers in drug
programs aim for total abstinence from all drug use for
their patients, others measure success by small
changes that show improvement in the conditions of
each addict's life. The originators of methadone programs, Drs. Marie Nyswander and Vincent Dole, have
had considerable experience in reducing doses of
methadone. In some cases, people have asked to have
their doses of methadone reduced to zero so that they
could eliminate taking the drug and live lives without
the nuisance of reporting to a clinic for supplies. Even
though these people had long since given up contacts
with drug pushers and had settled into warm family
relationships, good jobs, and comfortable life-styles,
the old craving and drug seeking behavior returned
from time to time. Many authorities are convinced
that the craving is a biological phenomenon rather
than a psychological urge. This idea is important
when one is considering social rehabilitation. If heroin
addiction is a metabolic disease, treatment may have
to be continued, much as insulin treatment is needed
throughout the life of a diabetic. Many authorities dis-
agree with this concept.

New research in the field of opiate receptors is
providing some important and exciting information in
the understanding of opiate addiction that seems to
support the above theory. The search for natural mor-

phinelike substances began in a few laboratories in different parts of the world in 1972. In late 1975, the search was successful, and morphinelike substances were extracted from the brains of animals in Scotland. Dr. Sol H. Snyder, Professor of Psychiatry and Pharmacology at Johns Hopkins University School of Medicine, is one of the early researchers in this field who is working with these natural opiates called endorphins that include molecules called enkephalins. One aim of Dr. Snyder's research is the discovery of relatively nonaddicting drugs that might serve as substitution drugs for heroin addicts.

The use of methadone as an addictive substitute for heroin has already been mentioned. Recently a drug known as LAAM (levo-alpha-acetyl-methadol), has been introduced in treatment clinics after much experimental testing. LAAM is longer-acting than methadone, lasting from seventy-two to ninety-six hours in most patients, but it, too, is addictive.

Mixing an antagonist similar to naloxone or cyclazocine with a substitute opiate similar to methadone, LAAM, or even newer experimental substitutes might lead to a nonaddicting drug with the properties that would help in relieving pain and treating heroin addicts.

Dr. Snyder reports that the new knowledge about the existence of opiate receptors in humans has led to renewed speculation that there may be a genetic basis, at least in part, for addiction. There might be a difference in the number or location of opiate receptors in different individuals that could have something to do with the variations in people's addiction potential.

A system of natural opiates appears to be involved in controlling people's moods in the face of stress. If this is so, abnormalities in the system could be expressed as disorders of mood, such as depression, or as abnormal sensitivity to pain. Dr. Avram Goldstein, director of the Addiction Research Foundation and professor of pharmacology at Stanford University, Palo Alto, California, an important researcher in this field, says one can even imagine that an abnormal endorphin or enkephalin system could play a role in increasing a person's vulnerability to heroin addiction. If such is so it might be that heroin would be a substitute for the substance they are missing. Much further research is needed to explore this exciting potential.

Dr. Theodore Cooper, Assistant Secretary for Health, told the Select Committee on Narcotics Abuse and Control, House of Representatives, on September 30, 1976, that the opiate receptor work being supported by the National Institute on Drug Abuse is clearly one of the most important scientific projects now being conducted in the United States. Dr. Cooper said that this exploration began by the discovery of particular sites within the brain that are receptors for opiate compounds. He believes that if the complex physiological interactions which occur at these sites can be understood, we will substantially increase our knowledge about why some persons become addicted to drugs and others do not, as well as adding to our understanding of the human brain.

There are many theories about heroin addiction. The conditioning theory of reinforcement and learning is one. Basically, this theory is based on the principle that most behavior whether good or bad is learned. Learned behavior is influenced by the consequences that follow it, so behavior that is pleasant is reinforced and behavior that is not pleasant is avoided. This is an oversimplification of the theory, but it presents the main idea. In the case of heroin addiction, heroin is considered as a positive reinforcer when it produces euphoria. Withdrawal symptoms represent a negative reinforcer and so do the anxiety and craving that follow withdrawal. The part played by the development of physical dependence and the termination of withdrawal by the further administration of heroin are easily explained by conditioning theory. But conditioning does not explain the cause and the motivation that underlie the first experimentation. It does not completely explain why heroin is so powerful in relieving whatever psychic pain made some heroin addicts try the drug or why there is an overwhelming need in some people to try it again. It does help to explain why constant cues in the environment in which the heroin was used reinforce the drug-using behavior.

There is an almost classic story about an ex-addict

who returned home from prison after five years. During the time in prison he was believed to be free of drug use. He did not crave heroin or think much about it. But when his bus entered his old neighborhood, the prisoner suffered withdrawal symptoms even though he was not drug-dependent, for this was familiar behavior for that environment.

It appears that craving for an addicting drug occurs principally when that drug is available. Studies of Vietnam veterans who used heroin overseas indicated that most of them used heroin only occasionally after returning to the United States, where the drug was not easily available. In a study involving 20,000 persons that was conducted over a twelve-month period, 10 percent remained addicts, and 80 percent said they still used heroin occasionally.

For a large number of addicts, heroin represents an attempt to cope, and/or a removal of conflict, and/or membership in a meaningful peer group. While there are many personality differences among addicts who choose the opiates, the great majority seem to come from family backgrounds where there was a high level of mistrust, where a parent was absent or did not function as a good role model, or where there were other problems that prevented the addict from sharing the normally valued roles of society. Even where the addict does share the normal values of society, cultural and personal means of attaining goals are commonly absent. Poor personal resources and limited chances for advancement play a large part in the adoption of a different set of values.

A new type of heroin addict is described as one with higher-than-average personal and social competence. This type of addict comes from a higher social and economic level and frequently sets goals that are unrealistically high. Failure to reach these goals has a detrimental effect on self-esteem, and heroin is used to escape the anxiety and depression that follow. Therapies that help the person to redefine goals or attain skills necessary to reach them have helped to increase self-esteem and reduce the need for drugs.

Heroin addiction appears to be closely related to social problems such as poverty, lack of education, lack of jobs, and subhuman housing. These have been called the fundamental cause of addiction. To eradicate addiction, many authorities believe one must eradicate the conditions that breed it. Few people question that the conditions mentioned above contribute to the need of many members of society to escape from their physical and psychic pain through drugs. But in addition to the work needed to improve conditions of society, help is needed now for vulnerable personalities in the far-from-perfect social conditions that exist today.

The roots of heroin addiction are many, and no matter which theory or group of theories about causes is correct, lack of funding presents obstacles for those who are coping with the prevention and treatment of addicts. When the court system puts thousands of addicts back on the streets without medical or psychological help, job training, or other rehabilitation, there is a cycle of use, arrest, release, use, arrest, release, etc. Certainly a variety and an expansion of treatment programs are needed so that different individuals can be matched to them even while the search continues for better ways of prevention and treatment.

For some people, a new way of life *can* be learned through counseling and/or self-help groups in which emotional maturity is developed. People who could not endure the ordinary frustrations of daily life have been known to mature out of their problems and learn to cope with stress in ways that do not involve drugs. While such success has been attained with highly motivated people, it may not work for others. Even though thousands of ex-addicts have been known to restructure their lives and live drug free for long periods of time, for others, opiate addiction is a chronic, relapsing illness that requires lifelong care.

For every success or partial success, in freeing heroin addicts from their dependence on this illegal drug and the hassle that goes with it, there is an advantage both to the patient and to society. For society, the advantage can be measured in various terms, including the idea that each recovered addict becomes an asset in preventing others from becoming addicts. Otherwise, s/he could be a focal point for the spread of further addiction. Dr. Sidney Cohen, former director of the Division of Narcotic and Drug Abuse of the National Institute of Mental Health, suggests that "when sufficient numbers of drug dependent people in a community are rehabilitated, it becomes possible to eliminate the spread of addictive drug use to new consumers."*

Drug Abuse and Alcoholism Newsletter, vol. VI, no. 4 (May 1977), p. 4.

If someone calls you an addict, you may or may not be flattered. Few people consider addiction as a way of gaining strength, but Dr. William Glasser, director of the Institute for Reality Therapy in California, has developed a concept of positive addiction. Addictions such as jogging, cycling, and meditation do not dominate the lives of the addicts, but are used consciously, or unconsciously, as a mental strengthening. Negative addictions, in contrast, involve abuse to the point where they interfere with a person's health, economic situation, or social adjustment. Negative addictions may dominate a person's life, or they may not. Replacing a negative addiction with a positive addiction may have its benefits in improved health and enjoyment of life. This may be especially obvious in the case of a person who gives up smoking so that s/he can pursue cycling without shortness of breath.

Consider the case of Keith, who cycles every day for about an hour. He goes along, letting his mind float free as he travels along the bike path for mile after mile. He rides for the pure joy of it, and he does not think of himself as a bike addict, although his family sometimes teases him by calling him one. Every day for the past four years, unless the weather was extremely unpleasant, Keith has rolled his bike out of the garage and pedaled for an hour. If snow covered the ground, or an illness kept him away from his daily ride, Keith felt a sort of pain. He missed the relaxed, trancelike state of mind that he experienced on his bicycle. Keith could not express the feeling very well, but he knew it was extremely pleasurable and relaxing.

What Keith experiences while riding his cycle has been referred to by Dr. Glasser as the P.A. (Positive Addiction) state, and it is difficult for anyone to describe. Attempting to create the feeling fails, since it is a passive state, but one can create the conditions in which it may happen. Usually these are conditions in which very little thinking takes place. A person is being noncritical, relaxed, and feels as if the mind is floating free.

Dr. Glasser believes that it takes a minimum of six months to develop positive addiction, and many people experiencing this kind of addiction believe that it may take up to two years.

Dr. Glasser has extensively explored the concept of positive addictions and found that there are six aspects to becoming positively addicted—all of them common to runners, cyclists, meditators, and others. Here are the criteria that an activity must meet to qualify: (1) it must be something in which you participate for about an hour each day; (2) it must be easy for you to do; (3) the activity must be one that you can do alone, without depending on others; (4) there must be value to you in what you are doing, whether that value is physical, mental, or spiritual; (5) you should expect to improve by participating in the activity, but you are the sole judge of it; (6) you must not be self-critical (a point which Dr. Glasser emphasizes). Competition or criticism from yourself or others can prevent the addicting quality for which you are searching.

Many joggers who become addicted to their sport begin running for physical fitness. The National Jogging Association recently estimated that 2 million Americans jog at least a half-hour a day, four days a week. Most start out gradually, after medical checkups to assure that they will be increasing their physical health rather than harming it. Those who jog regularly report more than an increase in physical health. In spite of coping with foot problems and other physical hazards, the feeling of euphoria is expressed by many who run daily. The feeling of self-confidence that comes after the first half-hour on the road is sometimes escalated into a sensation of omnipotence. Even people who have never heard of Dr. Glasser's theory refer to their jogging as their addiction.

Dr. Bernard Gutin, a professor of applied physiology at Teachers College, Columbia University, is a runner who has observed that creative solutions to problems are often reported by regular joggers. He compares the type of brain activity one experiences during the euphoria to that found in meditation—and meditation is considered the most popular form of positive addiction by Dr. Glasser.

Several years ago, Dr. Glasser placed a questionnaire in the magazine *Runner's World* to find out as much as he could about his theory of jogging and positive addiction. About seven hundred people replied, about 75 percent of whom had been running regularly for an hour, six days a week, for a year. They answered the following two key questions positively: "Do you suffer if you miss a run?" and "Do you always enjoy your run?" This reaction can be compared to withdrawal from another kind of addiction.

Many addicted runners talk about the rhythm of running. Some describe a psychological release that comes from the rhythm of what seems like perpetual motion. Aching calves and blistered soles are a small price to pay for the strength it brings to those who struggle through to the state of positive addiction. One runner who says he is tired during the first mile of any run claims that his subconscious takes over after that and his body functions without instructions from his mind. With his mind free to wander, he enjoys a state in which he considers his mind to be resting in a vacuum.

The feeling of euphoria that joggers experience may well be one of the reasons they are addicted to their sport. Certainly this feeling plays a part in the addictions to other experiences and substances mentioned in this book, even though some addictions involve only moderately pleasant feelings or relief from tension.

The workaholic has been called an addict, but his addiction is one in which tension, in the form of competition and excitement, seems to be part of the attraction. Perhaps you know someone who works much of the time and appears to be addicted to work or a sport. The person who is so dependent on work that it is a dominant part of life, and who cannot stop without feeling guilty or uncomfortable, is a typical addict. Guilt feelings when the person is not working may be considered a form of withdrawal. For some hard workers, especially those who work for the love of it, there is freedom and diversity in their jobs, and vacations are welcome. According to some theories, these workers may be different from the true work addict. Vacations are a problem for people who use work as an escape. They do not know how to unwind. Definitions of addiction and individual situations vary so much that the hard worker, or player, may or may not be considered an addict even when motives are considered. The same problem is true in many other cases. A person who watches television much of the time is called a television addict, unless that person is confined to bed and has little choice of other things to do. Certainly, there are many variables to take into account when defining an addict.

You may have heard about candy lovers who are "hooked on sugar" or people who are "chocaholics." One could make a long list of substances and experiences that qualify under broad definitions of addiction, but some common threads appear again and again. While each addict differs from every other even though they may share the same kind of addiction, the same descriptions can be heard again and again: The addiction is "something in which one can lose oneself . . . something I crave . . . relief from stress . . . a way to experience euphoria." Tolerance and withdrawal are common concerns of those trying to eliminate their addictions.

Professional workers note that many kinds of addictions have been reinforced by routines repeated thousands of times during a lifetime. Most addicts probably slip into a pattern of behavior through repeated experiences of finding relief from stress by that kind of behavior. Addicts may have a lifelong struggle with a craving for fattening foods, alcohol, nicotine, gambling, or other addictive substances or experiences. A common finding of low self-esteem has led professionals to believe that many addicts who engage in self-destructive behavior expect rejection and personal failure. Addiction has been called anger turned inward. No wonder the building of self-confidence and self-esteem are important elements in addiction therapy.

Very often if a person gives up one addiction, another is acquired as a substitute. Heavy smokers who break their habit commonly substitute extra food. They reach for a cookie instead of a cigarette. In a recent conference, researchers of drug abuse, alcoholism, cigarette smoking, and obesity crossed the boundaries of their own special subjects to study common factors in substance abuse and habitual behavior. They looked for common psychological, sociocultural, physiological, and economic factors in substance-abuse behaviors that are valued negatively by society. A wide range of questions was proposed, such as: Do different substances have different biochemical pathways? Are similar nerve pathways involved in similar addictive behaviors? Is there universal agreement among scientists and lawmakers about when and how the use of substances and behavioral practices becomes labeled as harmful, abusive, addictive, or compulsive? What are the private and social costs of addictive acts? What are the consequences of how society deals with varying forms of abuse and addiction? Is the addicted a compulsive individual, a person indulging in choice behavior, a criminal, or a victim of a health or disease disorder? The purpose of the conference was to gain insights that would help in decisions about what kind of research to pursue.

Many questions about addictive behaviors remain. The factors that contribute to addictions are so complex and varied that all of the answers may never be found. There are no simple answers for those who want to give up an addiction, change from one kind to another, or learn how to become positively addicted to a sport such as jogging or an experience such as meditation.

SOURCES OF FURTHER INFORMATION

Addiction Research
Foundation of
Ontario
33 Russell Street
Toronto, Canada M5S
2S1

Al-Anon Family Group
Headquarters, Inc.
(Including Alateen)
P.O. Box 182
Madison Square Station
New York, New York
10010
*Consult telephone book
for local groups*

Alcohol and Drug Abuse
Programs Association
of North America
1101 Fifteenth Street,
N.W.
Suite 204
Washington, D.C. 20005

Alcoholics Anonymous
World Services, Inc.
P.O. Box 459
Grand Central Station
New York, New York
10017
*Consult telephone book
for local groups*

American Cancer Society
219 East 42nd Street
New York, New York
10017

American Health
Foundation
1370 Avenue of the
Americas
New York, New York
10019

American Heart
Association
5415 Maple Street
Suite 221
Dallas, Texas 75235

American Lung
Association
1740 Broadway
New York, New York
10019

Drug Abuse Council
1828 L Street, N.W.
Washington, D.C. 20036

Gamblers Anonymous
P.O. Box 17173
Los Angeles, California
90017
*Consult telephone book
for local groups*

National Clearinghouse
for Alcohol
Information
P.O. Box 2345
Rockville, Maryland
20852

National Clearinghouse
for Drug Abuse
Information
P.O. Box 1908
Rockville, Maryland
20850

National Clearinghouse
for Smoking and
Health
Center for Disease
Control
Bureau of Health
Education
Atlanta, Georgia 30333

National Congress of
Parents and Teachers
700 North Rush Street
Chicago, Illinois 60611
For alcohol information

National Council on
Alcoholism
733 Third Avenue
New York, New York
10017
*Consult telephone book
for local chapter*

National Council on
Compulsive
Gambling
142 East 29th Street
New York, N.Y. 10016

National Organization
for the Reform of
Marijuana Laws
2317 M Street, N.W.
Washington, D.C. 20037

National Youth
Alternatives Project
1830 Connecticut
Avenue, N.W.
Washington, D.C. 20009

Benson, Herbert. *The Relaxation Response*. New York: William Morrow, 1975.

Blaine, Jack D., and Demetrios A. Julius, Eds. *Psychodynamics of Drug Dependence*. Rockville, Maryland: National Institute on Drug Abuse, Research Monograph No. 12, 1977.

Brecher, Edward M., and the editors of Consumer Union Reports. *Licit and Illicit Drugs: The Consumers Union Report*. Boston: Little, Brown, 1972.

Bruch, Hilda. *Eating Disorders: Obesity, Anorexia Nervosa, and the Person Within*. New York: Basic Books, 1973.

Diehl, Harold S. *Tobacco and Your Health: The Smoking Controversy*. New York: McGraw-Hill, 1969.

Fixx, James F. *The Complete Book of Running*. New York: Random House, 1977.

Gamblers Anonymous. Los Angeles, California: G.A. Publishing Company, third edition.

Glasser, William. *Positive Addiction*. New York: Harper and Row, 1976.

Glatt, M. M. *A Guide to Addiction and Its Treatment*. New York: John Wiley and Sons, 1974.

Grinspoon, Lester, *Marihuana Reconsidered*, Revised Edition. Cambridge, Mass.: Harvard University Press, 1977.

Hyde, Margaret. *Alcohol: Drink or Drug?* New York: McGraw-Hill, 1974.

————, *Brainwashing and Other Forms of Mind Control*. New York: McGraw-Hill, 1977.

————, Ed. *Mind Drugs*. Third edition. New York: McGraw-Hill, 1974.

Messolonghites, Louisa, Ed. *Alternative Pursuits for America's 3rd Century: A Resource Book on Alternatives to Drugs*. Rockville, Maryland: National Institute on Drug Abuse, 1974.

Milgram, Gail. *The Teenager and Smoking*. New York: Richards Rosen Press, 1972.

Peele, Stanton, with Archie Brodsky. *Love and Addiction*. New York: Taplinger, 1975.

Petersen, Robert C., and Richard C. Stillman. *Cocaine 1977*. Rockville, Maryland: National Institute on Drug Abuse, Research Monograph No. 13, 1977.

Platt, Jerome J., and Christina Labate. *Heroin Addiction*. New York: John Wiley and Sons, 1976.

Redd, William H., and William Sleator. *Take Charge: A Personal Guide to Behavior Modification*. New York: Random House, 1977.

Smart, Reginald G. *The New Drinkers: Teenage Use and Abuse of Alcohol*. Toronto, Canada: Addiction Research Foundation, 1975.

Willette, Robert, Ed. *Drugs and Driving*. Rockville, Maryland: National Institute on Drug Abuse, Research Monograph No. 11, 1977.

The Whole College Catalogue About Drinking. Rockville, Maryland: National Institute on Alcohol Abuse and Alcoholism, 1976.

INDEX